Sonoma Ghosts

By Carla Heine

Sonoma Ghosts is dedicated to You.

"I am half inclined to believe we are all ghosts, Mr. Manders. It is not only what we have inherited from our fathers that exists again in us, but all sorts of old dead ideas, and all kinds of old dead beliefs, and things of that kind. They are not actually alive in us, but there they are, dormant, all the same, and we can never be rid of them. Whenever I take up a newspaper, and read it, I fancy I see ghosts creeping between the lines. There must be ghosts all over the world. They must be as countless as the grains of sands. And we are so miserably afraid of the light, all of us."

GHOSTS, Act II
Henrik Ibsen

"JU-ON: a curse born of a grudge held by someone who dies in the grip of powerful angers. It gathers in the places frequented by that person in life, working its spell on those who come into contact with it, and thus creating itself anew."

JU-ON
Shimizu Tahi

"I am thy Father's spirit, doomed for a certain term to walk the night."

HAMLET, Act I
Shakespeare

5

TABLE OF CONTENTS:

A Circle In Time

Some people believe that as we go through life, the weeks, the months, the years, and the decades carry us downstream with the river of memory. Within the flow of our experience are the rough currents, the passing milestones, and the smooth steady progress toward the ever-closer sea.

The hard-packed sands of grit and courage fall back behind us, as we float forward away from our past, forward though our present, and forward into our future.

That isn't how it is with me. That's not how I experience time.

For me time streams, yes, but it streams around me. It goes forward, yes, but time slipstreams backward, too. Time divides in front of me, and time merges behind me.

In a constant present, I stand stock-still; the waters flow and change, and I endure, like a granite bedrock outcropping in the river of time.

With both feet firmly planted in the present, the past and the future flow around me. They ebb away into the distance like a much-loved season, and return again with the tides. They wax and wane with the cycles of the moon. They rise and set with the cycles of the sun.

The sparks of years, and decades, and centuries are starlight twinkles on the surface of eternity.

From my front door on Blue Wing Drive, my first kiss is only two blocks away. Two and a half blocks away is the old Simmons' Pharmacy. Mr. Simmons had the first car in Sonoma. Now it's Chico's dress store. My high-school sweetheart, Len Dillman, worked at the soda fountain in a white starch-pressed shirt, and he wore a white paper hat. He's dead, and I'm alive.

Len saved his pay, and bought me a dozen red long-stemmed roses on the 14th of every month. Not our anniversary; our university, we called it.

South on Second Street East, and left on Macarthur is Prestwood School, and here's where my father, Ed, drops me off every weekday morning at 8:30, gives me a kiss on the cheek, and says:

"Do good work."

Across the field, at Sonoma Valley Union High School, in a pink pleated angel dress chosen from the cover of Seventeen magazine, I graduate from Prestwood's eighth grade class of 1967.

From the edge of the Prestwood asphalt I look across the track, and dread P.E. for an entire summer, because Mrs. Gilcrest, the Prestwood English teacher, says they have co-ed P.E. and I am afraid I will have to shower naked in front of the boys.

Within one square mile around The Plaza, the year is simultaneously 1500, 1600, 1906, and 2001.

Within one square mile of where I now sit, I am a frustrated child who kicks at the dirt in an unsuccessful hunt for arrowheads; a lonely teen-ager experimenting with the complexities of cake-mascara; a young lady who takes afternoon naps with other girls clad in hot white cotton

10

camisoles and bloomers; a happy mystical Mission bride with 32 luminous flower girls; a devoted teacher; a well-known hostess; a chauffeur and historic tour guide to the paranormal world around us; a writer.

In 1972 I stand out on Eight Street East with the silent young boys of The Children's Telegraph. We watch both of our town's fat policemen rudely turn away the polite and glamorous Hungarian Gypsies and their horses and wagons, and rusted out station wagons, after 99 years of unanimous welcome and acceptance in Sonoma.

The center of this constant maelstrom is the present and my presence.

Friends, and loved ones break away from my concrete island in the present, eroded by steady currents and undercurrents, by whirlpools within whirlpools, by tides, and by counter-tides.

The trains, the hobos, and the Victorian ladies in their long beaded gowns are here, and gone. Around me, deep and wide, swirl narrow ribbons of life, and memory.

Time swirls, twirls, eddies, and spins back every nuance of light and dark from every moment of every day in every prismatic color of the spectrum.

Time is the rainbow-oil spread thin over star-lit puddles along the shores of an infinite number of other islands just like mine.

Time is the rainbow-oil spread thin over star-lit puddles along the curbs of the islands and the pumps at the Shell station on the corner of Broadway and Patten Street.

Bad Company

There were, and are, heroes in Sonoma. And there were, and are, any number of villains. Sometimes it's hard to tell them apart, and sometimes you have to look at them from different angles to see who is who. More often than not, there are heroes in the worst of us, and villains in the best of us.

But Sonoma has always had the best of the bad.

Early California towns have their histories. They have their secrets, too.

Certain times and certain places attract certain kinds of heroes and certain kinds of villains. The Blue Wing Inn is like that. The Blue Wing Inn has always been like that. It will be like that in the future, too.

Joaquin Murrieta was an Hispanic folk hero who took real and imagined actions on behalf of his people whenever they were oppressed unjustly.

Zorro, the fictional character, is based on Joaquin Murrieta's "subversive political activities", and on all of the heroic activities so generously attributed to him.

Senor Murrieta came to Sonoma often, and was a regular guest at The Blue Wing Inn, and other hotels, brothels, gaming places, and eateries.

In the Early California days, even though there was a price on his head, people gave him no trouble in Sonoma. They left him alone, so long as he didn't make trouble for them personally. He and his friend, Three Fingered Jack, had nothing to fear from the law in Sonoma for a long time. Both men spoke out for freedom for all regardless of race or creed.

Many people stepped into the role of Joaquin Murrieta in the 1850's, but not nearly as many have stepped into the role of Zorro.

Bernard Carr was Sonoma's earliest and best known Murrieta impersonator, and the Bancroft Library has a good collection of old photos that show him in and around The Blue Wing Inn. This one shows the original staircase, and there's an orb in the corner of the photo on the lower right.

People who are "not from here" always speculate about whether or not Captain Harrison Love, as seen on his prissy leopard skin saddle in "The Mask of Zorro", really did cut off the head of Joaquin Murrieta, and put it in a glass water jar full of whiskey.

14

People who are from here do not have to speculate.

Robert Parmelee authored "Pioneer Sonoma", and that is a book well worth buying if you can find a copy. Many old Sonoma stories came to him from talks he had with Lenore Franquelin, now Mrs. Galt Eliassen, who grew up on the Franquelin Farm down off Napa Street West, which is now a pleasant development nestled around the original Franquelin farmhouse and walnut orchards. Only now we all call it Franquelin Place.

Mr. Parmelee is a local attorney whose office is still on The Plaza just two doors North of the Sebastiani Theatre. Mr. Parmelee has the most extensive collection of early Sonoma slides and photographs of any private citizen.

I always wondered what possessed him to make a study of a subject that was neither lucrative, nor of much interest to anybody, especially in a town whose unavowed purpose was to sweep the most interesting facts about Sonoma under a tightly woven carpet of Victorian censorship.

Now, I follow haphazardly in his footsteps, and people wonder the same thing about me.

When the mood strikes him, Mr. Parmelee speaks at The Community Center, or for the Historical Society, or for the League for Historic Preservation, just like I do, only better, and differently.

Sometimes, he gives slideshows along with the lectures, and sometimes he simply lectures, but do not miss a chance to see him when the opportunity comes along, because none of us are getting any younger.

Beth Marie Deenihan went to one of his lectures at The Community Center in Andrews Hall. Mr. Parmelee spoke on a broad range of

Sonoma subjects, people, and events, and among them were the stories of Captain Harrison Love, and Joaquin Murrieta.

In the 1850's people all over California desperately needed a hero, especially the Spanish and Mexicans who were treated so badly by the American gringo conquerors during what Hispanic historians call "The American Invasion".

These abused victims were emboldened to stand up for their rights by the heroic actions of the original Joaquin Murrieta. With time his legend grew, as people who did things to protect themselves, their friends, and their families attributed their own deeds to Joaquin Murrieta.

Murrieta was said to be in Los Angeles committing one "crime" at noon, and then in San Francisco he was seen committing another "crime" at two o'clock, and he was often reported in two, or three, or even four or five places at once.

The American government in Sacramento did not want to draw attention to his alleged exploits by setting a reward for his capture, but it got to the point where somebody had to do something, because people were terrified, and they complained loudly, and publicly.

Finally, the citizens of California, under the Stars and Stripes, demanded aggressive action be taken immediately by their government.

Sacramento posted a reward, and in keeping with the political mood of the time, in Sonoma General Vallejo promised a $2000.00 reward himself; out of his own pocket.

To move things along quickly Vallejo called for Captain Harry Love, a mercenary soldier, Captain of the California Rangers, to whom he gave $1000.00 in gold, half the reward in advance, and the promise of the $1000.00 balance provided Love delivered proof of Murrieta's death.

Murrieta wasn't wanted dead or alive.

Murrieta was wanted dead.

Captain Love gathered a small and unsavory entourage of 20 mercenary Rangers, rode out of Sonoma, and headed for Clear Lake. After several days of roaming around without any sign of the famous bandit, they came across five random ranch hands who were encamped for the night on the Clear Lake Ranchero.

Without one Spanish speaker among his men, and not a Spanish speaker himself, Captain Love somehow ascertained that one or more of these men were named Joaquin; a name that's as common in Spanish as John is in English.

At Love's command the mercenaries killed all five men, and Love himself decapitated of one of them, and bagged that head to use as physical proof that Joaquin Murrieta was indeed dead.

Captain Love brought the head in its burlap bag back to the pueblo Sonoma. He took it to the Blue Wing Inn where he collected money from a number of men who had bet against his finding and killing Joaquin Murrieta.

From the Blue Wing, the news spread like wildfire through California.

At the Blue Wing Inn, Love had the head put into a large glass water jar, had it filled with whisky, not brandy as some claim, and then sealed the lid to the jar with melted candle wax.

Harrison Love then took the head in the jar one block down East Spain Street to the US. Cavalry officers quartered in the Ray-Nash Adobe, where I grew up, and collected his winnings from the officers there who had also bet against him. Love was not a popular man there.

This done, Captain Love went to see Vallejo, to collect from the General the balance of the $2000.00 reward.

The newspapers were all notified, the death and decapitation of the infamous bandit was in all the papers, everybody felt much safer, and the California comptroller's office wrote Harry Love a check.

Problem solved.

Or was it?

The head was of little use, or interest to Captain Love after he had collected the $2,000.00 reward, and the unknown amount of money from his bets. It was all ill-gotten gains.

Captain Love sold the head, and the jar, for $35.00 in gold to one of his subordinate California Rangers, a man by the name of Billy Henderson.

Thirty-Five dollars was a good investment when you consider it cost one dollar per person to see the head when it was on display in Stockton, San Jose, San Diego, Santa Barbara and Los Angeles.

We know the head traveled on display throughout California, and until 1906 it was on permanent display at Jordan's Museum in San Francisco.

The State of California has a brass plaque in Arroyo de Cantua that is a lot like the plaques in Sonoma, and probably just like the ones all over the state. It looks authentic, but the facts it states are based on iffy local say-so and official military records. It would cost too much to have them all corrected.

Billy Henderson took his purchase there, because that is the official place where the official Joaquin Murrieta officially met his death.

The head was exhibited all over California, and somehow the alleged hand of Three Fingered Jack Mansong, Murrieta's best friend and cohort, ended up in the jar, too. Jack Mansong was a legend in Sonoma for his oratory.

Murrieta's sister came to see it, and she said that this head was most definitely not the head of her brother Joaquin.

I believe her. I myself would certainly recognize the head of either of my brothers, decapitated and swollen with whiskey in a glass jar, or not!

The jar and its dubious contents were "presumed lost in the 1906 Earthquake".

Just like the original Bear Flag, with its piggy-bear, and the blatant misspelling of the word "Republic".

Just like the 17 miles of brick-lined tunnels under Sonoma.

Just like My Aunt Fanny.

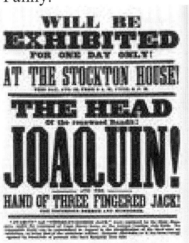

At the end of the Community Center lecture in Andrew's Hall, Beth Marie Deenihan went up to say hello to Mr. Parmelee, and thank him, and there was a whole family there talking to him. One of the women was crying.

They were thanking Mr. Parmelee, and as Beth Marie waited she heard them explain why his lecture meant so much to them personally.

Their family ranch was the Clear Lake Ranchero and Captain Love had killed five of their family's innocent ranch-hands in cold blood, decapitating one of them.

As if that were not bad enough, Harrison Love was guilty of the grand deception in which he had passed the head off to the world as that of the famed bandit Joaquin Murrieta.

Politically expedient as this deception was in calming the fears of the new American Gringos, and despite the added prestige and respect this false victory gave to the California Rangers, the burden of truth lay heavily on the consciences of the Clear Lake Ranchero Family and their vaqueros.

This had been a deep dark secret in their family, a shameful secret, which they kept from the world for over a hundred years, because they were afraid to go against the unscrupulous Captain Love, and the General, Guadelupe Vallejo, and his brother Salvador Vallejo, and the machinery of the entire California government.

This family had a deep, and rational fear of the Vallejo Brothers because they led the Bloody Island Massacre in which 800 men heavily under the influence of the sacred hallucinogens were burned to death in their ritual sweat-lodge in the middle of Clear Lake.

Then, when they were defenseless, 1600 Indian women and children were taken, by force, against their will, back to Sonoma to serve as slaves on the Vallejo estates.

Miss Natalia Vallejo stated that her father was not in attendance at the Bloody Island Massacre with her uncle, because her mother had been ill all morning and "Father had stayed home to attend her that day".

This is a child's nursery tale born of the Spanish aristocracy's traditional belief that one's children should never have to see or hear about the things adults must do.

This was deeply ingrained in the Vallejo men, as deeply ingrained as their belief in Jesus Christ.

But in Andrew's Hall on the night of Mr. Parmelee's lecture, there were any number of people who knew the truth behind both these well-kept California secrets.

For the Clear Lake Rancho family descendants to hear Mr. Parmelee openly tell both these true stories, freed them of their shameful burden at long last. The openly spoken truth both vindicated, and absolved this great generational guilt.

And Captain Love was finally revealed as the scoundrel he really was.

So eight years later I'm cruising along in Lola, my Little Old Lincoln Automobile, a silver 1988 Presidential stretch limousine, with a Twilight Tour group from Sonoma, and we are doing the Ghosts and Legends tour of 13 haunted buldings and historic sites.

We park in front of Andrews Hall, at The Community Center where this lecture took place, and we're exchanging information on the whole Captain Love and the jar story.

"They say it was destroyed in the fire after the 1906 Earthquake." I tell my guests.

"But it wasn't." says one of the men in the back.

"What do you mean?" I ask him, and I turn around in the driver's seat to look at him face to face.

"It wasn't destroyed in the 1906 Earthquake." says my guest, and he grins.

"How do you know it wasn't?" I ask him, now eye to eye.

"I've seen it." he says, still grinning.

"No way!" I exclaim. He had my total attention now, and my internal lie-detector was on red alert.
.

A tid-bit of information like this, if true, is a major event for me.

"Yes! Way!" he says happily, with total confidence. "My mother used to shop at this antique store in Santa Rosa. One day we were there with her and Dad, and the owner asks if we wanted to see something special; something secret. And we're all, 'Yeah. Sure.' So he locks the front door, and pulls this big glass jar out from under the counter. And there it was."

"What did it look like?" I asked.

"Like a head in a jar." he says. "With a bunch of brown liquid. Actually it was pretty gross. I can't believe I forgot about it until just now, but I saw it with my own eyes."

"Was the hand in the jar?" I asked.

"You mean the hand of Three Fingered Jack? I don't know about the hand. I didn't see the hand myself, but I saw the head." he says.

I can tell he's telling me the truth.

"Where was this place?" I ask.

"On Franklin," he says, "in Santa Rosa. You know Santa Rosa?"   23

"I know where Franklin Avenue is."

"Near Memorial Park."

"On the way to Sutter Hospital?" I ask.

"On the other side."

"Is it still there?"

"The head?" he asks.

"No, the store." I say.

"I don't know."

It is funny, the stuff you forget from your childhood until somebody or something jogs your memory, and boom, suddenly there it is, all in one piece, like a hologram.

When a memory like that comes back like that for me, it brings everything else with it.

"We used to hunt for that jar in my parents' house, and in the Blue Wing Inn." I told him.

"Like a game? Like capture the flag?" he asks.

"Not exactly." I answer dryly.

It was no game. Our parents' new house and the Blue Wing Inn were part of history, not some made-up story. Besides, our great-great-grandfather Frederick had our great grandfather's best friend's head chopped off, and put in a glass water jar next to our great grandfather's bed. He ordered his son to leave it there until the day he died.

24

His father also ordered the friend's headless body to be left outside his son's window until the carcass rotted into the mud.

The whole head-in-a-jar thing was part of our family history to Eddie and me.

Eddie and I hunted for Captain Love's wax-sealed glass jar with the head that was not that of Joaquin Murrieta. We tapped on the three-foot thick adobe walls seeking out the hollow places, which most original adobe owners used as hidey-hidey holes, and safe-keeps.

We banged on the wood panels of the West Wing addition at 205 East Spain Street, upstairs and downstairs, in the attic, and in the crawl spaces under the eaves, and under the stairs.

We crept on knees and elbows through all the attics of both adobes, yanked out square-headed iron nails, pulled away loose boards under, and pushed in the slat-backs of all the closets.

We shoved our heads through a hundred years of ropey cobwebs; our eyes jammed shut against the mummy dust. We ripped out wads and wads of crumbly yellow newspaper, which Bill Black crammed between the studs for cheap insulation.

That was long time ago, but only two blocks away.

Eddie and I didn't have much information to go on, but we knew about the bets. And we knew how people in Sonoma buried true information in the rubble of the 1906 Earthquake.

Eddie and I figured the best place to look for Captain Love's jar was where we knew it had been twice, at least, already. We figured third time is the charm. Eddie and I never entirely gave up the search, and we never, ever, gave up hope.

Today I have more clues than anybody else in town, and now that we have more have more clues, maybe we can track down the man from the antique store on Franklin Avenue in Santa Rosa, and get him to donate the jar to the as yet non-existent Blue Wing Inn Museum.

Eddie's dead, now. It is 2008, and Eddie's been dead, now, for for almost 40 years.

Bartholomew Park Winery

If you go East, away from The Plaza, on Spain Street, you will dead end on Fourth, where the old train depot for the Sebastiani Cannery and the Sebastiani Winery isn't any more.

Turn left, and go up Fourth Street past the Sebastiani Winery, past the row of flagpoles with the Seven Flags of Sonoma on your right, and take the first right hand turn. This will put you on Lovall Valley Road.

This is the same path Colonel Jonathan Drake Stevenson took in 1862 when his secret mission for the Civil War was to round up and kill the last of the Sonoma Indians. Stevenson's mission was a well-kept secret for the most part, but not in Sonoma where Stevensons' son was killed.

In Sonoma, you can't just ride your high horse into town with 20 men and eight Gatlin guns, round up 7,500 men, women, and children, drive them out of town like a big herd of cattle, and kill them all without being noticed.

Even if they are Indians.

Go straight on Lovall Valley Road, but watch the speed bump; it's new and some of us still find it pretty funny to sit under the trees on the edge of the vineyard at the picnic table, so we can watch unconscious speeders whack their undercarriages and rattle their teeth.

When Lovall Valley dead ends at the three way stop, go left, and then take the middle of the three roads in front of you up Castle Road to Bartholomew Park Winery. After a dozen acres of vineyard, you'll see a nice white building reminiscent of Monticello (a great place for a big party with an excellent wood dance floor and marvelous acoustics).

This is the Haraszthy Villa, but it is not the original Haraszthy Villa; the original Haraszthy Villa burned down by accident. Mrs. Bartholomew built this one as a memorial to her husband, Frank.

Drive along with the reconstituted villa on your left, and you will see an oak studded knoll up ahead, and a long two-story Spanish style building to your right.

Park anywhere.

The adobe look is really achieved with stucco and white paint, but the red Spanish tiles are the real thing, and so is the crest. The wine here is very good, with a broad selection of varietals from the same house. You could live well on Bartholomew Park wines, and unless you have an undeveloped pallate, or a limited imagination, you will be happy for a hundred years.

28

Is it haunted? No doubt about that.

Every October they have an event here called "Sips and Spirits". The event started as a séance with the staff and a few mediums, and I was invited to be an objective witness, but to tell the truth, I was scared to go. I was Chicken. Brock-Brock.

I don't seek weirdo stuff out. I just remember and report it. I'm an accidental psychic.

It would have been nice to make everyone happy by saying "Yes, I shall be delighted to attend your séance. Thank you for inviting me." But I was flat-out scared to go. Scared to go, and scared to say no, so I waited to RSVP.

The quandary solved itself, as so many quandaries will, if you can sit tight and do nothing. That nice ex-Marine from Manhattan, John Mirsberger, invited me to spend two weeks in Kauai with him, at which point, the real séance of six mutated into a faux séance of twenty-five.

Aloha!

I never had to say a word to the winery after all.

The winery decided to go with the flow, opened the seance to the public as an entertainment event, and charged admission.

Over a hundred people showed up that first night, and the winery served wine and cheese, exotic Inca chocolates gilded with 24 karat gold, and Sonoma French bread.

Now it's an annual event, and a whole series of psychics come. This year the famous ghost expert and author Jeff Dwyer was the keynote speaker.

Jeff has written a whole series of ghost hunter's guides, and his latest book is the Ghost Hunter's Guide to The Wine Country. Jeff Dwyer lived in Sonoma until recently, but we met when he was researching Sonoma's ghosts for his book. He was a real inspiration to me, because if he could do it, I could do it.

I like Jeff Dwyer's book, especially the part about the haunted locations in Sonoma that are open and accessible to the public. Jeff's writing style is clean-cut and straight forward. It's strange to see town secrets in print. But having been only one of his resources, I can't tell what came from whom.

It's enlightening and puzzling at the same time.

With my information I know who said what when and where, plus what they were wearing, eating, and drinking, and usually with or without whom they are sleeping.

Jeff, and Jackie from SPIRIT (Sonoma Independent Research Investigative Team; online at www.sonomaspirit.com), got to scope out Bartholomew Park Winery two weeks before the sipping spirits event.

They wanted to get EVPs (Electronic Voice Phenomena, or Electronic Voice Patterns). Jeff and I both know what a gift Jackie has for getting outrageous EVPs. We think that the spirit of the person making the EVPs has a lot to do with how well the EVPs come out.

There is a ton of hard scientific evidence to support our theory.

The results are on their respective websites. One sounds like someone talking in an unknown language, another is definitely someone playing mindlessly with a piano, an upright by the sound of it, not the grand piano that presently sits in the main room.

The weirdest EVP is definitely flutes; maybe reed flutes; maybe water gourd medicine flutes which are the North American equivalent to the terra cotta pottery ChiCha medicine flutes in Peru, which people often mistake for water pitchers, or small jugs.

The Bartholomew Park Winery was a home for wayward women, unwed mothers-to-be, prostitutes, drug addicts, and destitute women from the lowest streets in San Francisco, with the occasional disgraced daughter of a wealthy couple thrown in to give birth and return from the country without the baby and resume life as a born again virgin.

Babies born out of wedlock here were often placed with adoptive parents in Sonoma, and nearly all of them grew up none the wiser. After losing their babies, one way or the other, these women were returned to San Francisco to their respective neighborhoods and lifestyles. Such was life in those days.

Miserable as it seems, at least at the "Hospital" they had work as dairymaids. They were not paid, but they were fed, and housed, and clothed. Plus which, they had a real medical doctor in attendance when their time came.

It really was a much better arrangement than confinement at the Sonoma Asylum for the Insane, and you knew, at least, that your baby would be adopted by a real family from town; not just fed into the population of lunatics to live out their entire lives in a madhouse.

In its present incarnation as a family winery, the building with its museum and grounds beautifully maintained, enjoys its highly elevated sunny location, and a sunny outlook for its future. There is a sunny disposition among the staff, too. It's a great winery for family picnics, and you can hike the property, and see the Indian quarry, the cougar cave that served Chief of Chiefs Sum Yet Ho as a private place for prayer and meditation, and if you are intrepid, you can hike to the site of the Chinese settlement where 8,900 Celestials lived at the top of Castle Canyon.

You can see Mount Tamalpais from the top of Castle Canyon. But even the view from the parking lot of Bartholomew Park Winery is spectacular.

Bartholomew Park Winery hosts all kinds of special events. Sometimes they have book-readings there at night with authors who read their own work. These are wine and cheese events with hard thin-sliced French sourdough baguettes, and soft ripe cheeses with soft ripe French names. Reader's Books from East Napa Street hosted the last one I went to.

It was at night, and at night, in the dark, Bartholomew Park Winery is eerie in the extreme. Inside as well as out. There was a big tree by the front door. That tree is so strong in my memory that I cannot remember the entry walk without it.

There was an old story from a long way back about a man who was handed a rope, and then he hung himself from that tree. He never moved on, and he never came down from the tree. It's a legend, and I don't know if it is true. I honestly can't remember if the tree is still physically there, or not. If it is, it is. If it is not, then it was.

Some places have natural ambiance. Some places acquire ambiance. And some have ambiance thrust upon them. Bartholomew Park Winery has cases in point for all three.

As you enter the building, which was originally built by the State of California as an annex to the State hospital system, there is a wide wooden door with cast iron hardware and medieval studded nails. It opens smoothly, and it's heavy and thick. The front door is not made to keep someone or something out; it's made to keep someone or something in.

This door swings inward, which is not in compliance with modern safety, or fire codes. Public buildings are supposed to open outward, so in case the people inside panic, the door will still open, even if everyone presses the full weight of their bodies against it. Doors in that open inward are death traps waiting to snap shut. In the event of a panic, for whatever the reason, the weight of numerous bodies makes it impossible to open.

When the winery is open to the public and the door is open, you cannot see the secret door in the wall behind it. This secret door leads to a tight curl at the top of a small concrete staircase. Follow the stairs down, and you will find a cold narrow hallway with one naked light bulb overhead. This underground hall leads directly to the morgue.

34

There are a number of doorways off the hall where the winery stores wine for customers. But unlike a newspaper morgue, the winery morgue is not only a storage place for unused inventory. This morgue is a real, actual, once upon a time, morgue.

The stairway is too narrow and steep for a coffin, and unlike the Vallejo house's main staircase, there is no coffin corner to make it possible. Instead, there is a coffin chute, which was cast right into the concrete foundation when this large two-story structure was built.

The coffin chute leads up to the surface outside. Corpses of the departed could be stored in the dark cool of the underground morgue until the groundskeeper on the premises could build the coffins. The chute is very narrow, and it is easy to see how small and pitiful the plain wood coffins were. They were almost as small and as pitiful as the occupants themselves.

"One man took a photo in the morgue, and one of the old coffins showed up in the picture." a winery employee told me.

"The morning after the Sips and Spirit's night, one of the guests was standing in front of me at the tasting room bar," another employee said, "and he was shoved in the back from behind. He slammed into the edge of the bar, and his face turned totally white."

See what I mean? All those mediums and psychics at that event stir up the paranormal pot. Same thing happens at the Sonoma Hotel every time they paint or redecorate, but that's mostly just Fred. But there are some heavy-duty spirits at this winery, and not all the life forms on the grid are human, or sympathetic. Call me old-fashioned. Call me chicken. Brock-Brock. I don't go to séances. I don't take chances.

At least at the Sonoma Hotel there have only been a few deaths on the premises. Death passed through the Sonoma Hotel casually, from time to time. Death was a steady resident, a member of the family, during Bartholomew Park Winery's original incarnation.

Despite the presence and the necessity for a morgue, there is no cemetery on the premises. No known cemetery, that is. Like most

Sonoma protestants and paupers, these poor maids and their dead babies were buried in the graveyard down on East Macarthur, which was also an original Sonoma Indian burial ground created by the Europeans for victims of the smallpox epidemic of 1937, 1938, and 1939.

Don't bother to look for their markers. There aren't any, and the majority of the Macarthur Street cemetery graves rest in peace under the Ledson "starter-castles" on Denmark Street. The Chinese section is under Prestwood.

One summer three of those big houses burned to the ground within a week of each other.

Have you ever seen an episode of the TV Western series "Gun Smoke"? Remember Miss Kitty? The Sheriff, Matt Dillon, was in love with Miss Kitty. She owned the bar. If you remember Miss Kitty, add red-hair to those cat eyes, and make them emerald green. Give her skin like English roses done in Dresden porcelain, and a figure like lady in the painting that used to hang over the Sonoma Hotel Bar, and you'll have a conservative approximation of my friend Susan Scarborough.

Susan is from here.

She is also a licensed non-denominational minister who performs weddings and has contacts and influence throughout Sonoma Valley.

Susan and I did a decade of Nutcrackers together with the Sonoma Ballet Conservatory under the direction of Beth Marie Deenihan. Susan and I were Mothers at the big Christmas party in the First Act. Susan is smart, kind, positive, and generous with her time and energy. She is far more practical than I will ever be, and she has a backbone like tempered steel.

She has a ready laugh, and wise eyes.

Susan is "Town". Being "Town" is like being "from here", only closer to the Plaza; basically Fourth Street East to Fourth Street West, from Blue Wing Drive to Patten Street.

Susan and I took some of Susan's friends for a Twilight Tour in Lola. Whatever Lola wants, Lola gets. Susan told me then and there in the limousine that she had once worked at Bartholomew Park Winery. Susan was the first person to tell me about the cardboard cat effect.

Many other people, too, not just Susan, have experienced the cardboard cat effect.

Every winery has at least one winery cat. If you want a winery cat, just build a winery. One will show up right away.

A winery is a great place to be a cat. You get the best of both the indoor, and the outdoor life. People come, and love you up, and they go away, and leave you to your freedom, and they feed you. Winery cats are fat, and happy.

The original Buena Vista winery cats were Russian Blues. They were escapees from The Castle. The Bartholomew Park Winery cat is fat and happy, but on occasion, usually when the staff is closing for the night, he is literally one scared-stiff cat. It comes over him, all of a sudden, and he just turns to cardboard.

It's like live rigor mortis. You can pick him up just as if he is made out of papier-mâché. The stiff spinal arch stays in his back, and his normally sharp squinty eyes stare out wide open, but he is completely blind. He won't even blink. His legs are stiff as a board. His tail sticks

37

straight up, and his fur sticks straight out in clumps, like a movie rat groomed with Vaseline.

To pick him up is the only thing to do; you can't leave him like that. You have to pick him up and take him outside. He won't feel like a live cat at all. Live cats, when you pick them up, most of their bones melt, and they are all soft, warm, and pliable. Something makes this cat feel more like a taxidermy specimen. Full of sawdust. Hard. Dry. Cold from the inside out.

Once you get him outside the building, you set him down on his rigid little paws, and wait. You have to wait about one full minute. Then the cat shudders, shakes himself out like a dog after a bath, and flies off into the night like the proverbial bat out of Hell.

They tell me the first time it happens to you is the worst, but after that you never get used to it.

One night Susan was the last to leave the winery building, and she had to get the kitchen ready in advance the night before, for a big wedding party. The bakers were to come early the next morning, so she put a big bag of white flour up on the counter for them.

The winery cat was already outside, so she locked up, and went home. Last out and first in is a guarantee of good luck in a theatre. Susan was the last out that night, and at five in the morning she was the first in.

Was Susan lucky?

You tell me.

Susan unlocked the heavy front door, and she walks back to the kitchen. She turns on the overhead lights, and she sees the entire bag of flour up-ended onto the middle of the kitchen floor tiles. The heap in the middle of the floor is a mountain of fine snow-white powder, and the flour around it spreads out until the resulting volcano is over three feet in diameter.

There are no paw-prints, no shoe marks anywhere around the exterior, or the interior of the mountain of flour. The place had been locked down tight all night, and nobody entered the building before Susan.

Nevertheless, right smack in the middle of the flour volcano is a pair of tiny footprints less than four inches long.

Baby-foot prints.

Susan looks at the baby footprints, turns around, switches off the lights, relocks the front door behind her, and walks out to her car where she waits for the wedding bakers, and the winery staff to arrive.

She doesn't hang around in the spooky building all alone waiting to see if Rosemary's Baby shows up.

I've always admired Susan. Susan is practical. Susan doesn't work there anymore.

When I see something that far off the wall, I don't hang around, or form a committee to discuss it, or organize an informal amateur séance. I run. I make tracks. I boogie like a bat out of Hell.

I have at least as much sense as the winery cat.

Mrs. Bartholomew put the Buena Vista Rancho, which includes 75 acres and the Bartholomew Park Winery, into a special land trust, so someday it will all become part of a public park for everyone to enjoy and appreciate. She and Mr. Bartholomew saw the way Sonoma's been going, and they were not impressed.

It was Mr. and Mrs. Frank Bartholomew who coined the phrase "promiscuous building. '

If you live in Sonoma, sooner or later you will find yourself wondering if we are that. Are we just a bunch of destructive creators who'd like to chop up all the land, and the space above it from the ground to the moon, into ten by ten squares to be sold as condominiums, piecemeal, to the highest bidders?

George Washington said: "Few people have the virtue to resist the highest bidder."

If what Mr. and Mrs. Frank Bartholomew said is true, then they are right.

We are condo sluts.

Buena Vista Winery

The Buena Vista Winery has two regular ghosts, 19 Chinese tunnel ghosts, the ghost of Chief Solano, and one something-or-other, which I hope never to not see again, especially in the dark at night when I am alone.

Count Agoston Haraszthy founded California's oldest winery, on a Spanish land grant, which was a double dowry from the father-in-law of the two robust young Hungarian sons he married off to the daughters of General Mariano Guadalupe Vallejo.

Known today as the "Father of Modern Viticulture", Count Haraszthy underwrote the winery with $50,000 in gold which he came up with out of nowhere; gold that was surely not scavenged from the soot and ash off the rooftops of the San Francisco smelts where he worked as the poorly paid assayer of the San Francisco Mint.

Count Haraszthy resigned from that position of fiduciary trust after an audit by the board of directors who asked him how it was that the gold, which arrived there to be smelted, actually weighed less after the smelting.

Agoston Haraszthy patiently explained that in the smelting process small amounts of gold dust flew up through the chimneys and landed on the roof with the rest of the soot and ash from the fires used to melt the gold. He took them up to the roof, and showed them fine sprinkles of gold dust upon the soot and ash. They were satisfied. He then resigned, ostensibly affronted by their audacity and lack of confidence in his integrity, and retired to Sonoma.

Although the Count employed mostly Chinese workers, he also employed local European workers, and he was so well regarded that out of respect to his title, his money, and his native Hungary, the Gypsy caravans were welcome in Sonoma, and participated annually in the Harvest, and Vintage Festival Parades for 99 years.

The long line of huge eucalyptus trees that run along Old Winery Road attest to Vallejo and Haraszthy's original plan for the railroads to go right up to the winery's doorstep. But that railroad spur was never built.

Eucalyptus trees were imported from Australia and planted in advance. The idea, which looked good on paper, was to give the trees five years to grow, by which time the coolies and the rail would arrive, and the trees would be big enough to chop into railroad ties. These trees had provided sturdy ties for Australia's rails, but unbeknownst to anyone in Washington DC, the Australians aged their downed wood five years to make it hard enough to hold the spikes. Polk and Lincoln didn't have five years.

So these advance efforts on behalf of the transcontinental railroads were in vain, as expensive and labor intensive as they were. Too bad.

The little town of Buena Vista is now only on the oldest maps, but if you stop and look around the four way intersection at Lovall Valley Road and Seventhth St. East, you will see the dock house which was the heart of this once busy little center of international commerce.

Buena Vista had a permanent population of 800 souls, and flat bottom boats brought all kinds of goods in from the tall ships that made port at the Embarcadero de Sonoma. The town of Buena Vista serviced not only the winery and the families who lived there, but also the 8,900 Celestials who lived up at Castle Canyon's Chinese settlement.

It is from the Chinese settlement on the original Buena Vista property that a labyrinthine underground city with 17 miles of brick tunnel begins.

The history of these forgotten ballrooms and hallways has now passed from living memory in Sonoma. This underground city has joss houses, opium dens, a jail, gaming rooms and even prostitutes.

This was necessary to protect the Chinese from death at knifepoint or by gunshot. In Sonoma, it was always open season for the Chinese.

Other tunnels the Chinese had secretly dug under the Mayacamas mountain range allowed them to increase their incomes quietly and significantly.

These tunnels led directly into the back of silver and quicksilver mines along the Silverado Trail in Napa Valley.

By working above in Sonoma by day, and working in the Silverado mines by night, the industrious Chinese could pay off their indentured contracts, buy back their freedom more quickly, and move into profit.

Only the Chinese themselves knew the extent of this underground world they had created. Almost all Chinese cultural aspects of Sonoma's history have yet to be disclosed to the public.

Many access points are on private property, but the City of Sonoma uses some of them almost daily, for elecrrical conduits and travel.

"You go underground in your work for the City." I said to a friend of mine who no longer works for the City. "Did you ever run into any of those old Chinese tunnels we used to hear about when we were kids?"

"Oh, Carla." he says, and shakes his head like he is saying yes. "You don't want to go down there."

"But you have been in them." I said. "Right?"

"It's dirty down there. It's full of cobwebs and spiders."

"I'm not afraid of spiders. I grew up with two brothers. Remember?"

"Yeah, but it's dirty down there." As if when we grew up in Sonoma, there was no such thing as dirt.

"Tell me about it." I prompted.

"I will tell you this," he says to me in a confidential tone, "When I first started working for the City, the man who trained me said 'They can't fire me now, and they can't take away my pension.' He had two weeks to go before retirement, and he said, 'You gotta see this.' So we got two Coleman lanterns, and a couple of flashlights, and we put out the orange cones, and pulled up a manhole cover, and went down the hole. There were concrete tubes, and electrical wires and lights for awhile, but then we came to a little wooden door about so high."

He indicates a height of about four feet with his hand.

"It wasn't even locked, or anything, and he just opens the door, and we went in. There were no lights, so we lit the lanterns, and we had to duck because the roof was low, but we went down about 120 feet at a ten degree angle."

My mind reached back uselessly, a memory octopus with tentacles shot full of Novocain and groping for a Euclidian geometry formula I had known, but all I got was jumbled pictures of Mr. Kruljac with his fingers on my thigh as he measured the distance between the top of my knee and the hem of my mini-skirt while I stood on a chair in front of my high school Algebra class wondereing if my underpants showed.

So I gave up trying to figure out how deep that would be, and pulled my attention back to hear what my friend was saying about his rare adventure into the brick maze of Chinese tunnels.

"We came out into this round room about 30 feet in diameter, and it was all lined in brick, and it had a domed ceiling that came down at the sides and stopped about four feet above the floor."

"Was there a wall there?" I asked.

"No. Doors. Wood doors. About four feet high, and two and a half feet wide, and they were all carved. Really nicely carved. Somebody did a good job on these. They had flowers and vines, with leaves, and birds. Like the front of the old wine casks at Sebastiani Winery. And there were thirteen of them. All around the room. No walls. Just doors."

I pondered this. Thirteen is a lucky number in the Chinese tradition. Lucky for gambling. Lucky for love. Lucky for business. Lucky for pleasure.

"They had girls' names written on them." He raised his eyebrows at me with great significance. "In English." he added. "But they were Chinese names, like, Princess Tiger Lily, and Jade Snow."

My mind will sometimes make useless contributions when there is an information void, or a lack of known data. It pulls whatnots out of the catchall drawer in my subconscious. Then it tries to sound really helpful.

'Jade Snow' it says to me in response to my friends' statements, 'is a world-renowned Chinese potter from San Francisco. And Princess Tiger Lily is from Peter Pan, and she's an Indian. She's not Chinese.'

I don't know how you handle it when this happens, but I take my cue from the Saint Andrews' golf pros. I play through.

'Jade Snow never came to Sonoma, and even if she's a hundred years old by now, she's still not old enough to have been here in 1860, or 1870.' I told my mind. "And Princess Tiger Lily is a fictitious character from the mind of J. M. Barrie, not a real Indian. And even if she was a real Indian she wouldn't be down there anyway, because…"

'…Chinese and Indians don't mix.' My mind sometimes finishes my sentences for me. Does yours do that?

"Did you open any of the doors?' I asked my friend.

He rolls his eyes at me as if to say, 'Duh, Carla! You think we'd get all the way down there, and not open the doors? Hello?'

"What was behind them?" I ask.

"Nothing. A cave. But nothing. Just a hole in the dirt."

"What else was down there?"

One of the advantages of living in the same town for forty years, you get to know people's habits.

This guy probably still has the first fishhook he ever made out of his little brother's diaper pin. We both collect old bottles, rusted out machine parts, and useless square nails handmade by long dead Sonoma blacksmiths.

"Broken pieces of white clay pipes. You know." We were both seeing the white clay pipes like the Amish use, the ones that break if you look at them. "Sardine tins." Probably from Cannery Row in Monterey. The Chinese made the tins into oil lanterns and wind chimes, and used them as little frying pans. "Checker boards on top of chicken crates. Long narrow boards down by the floor, held up off the floor at both ends with stacked bricks." To sit on, or to lie on probably.

"What do you think?" I asked him.

"What do you think?" he asks me.

We gave each other the "You think what I think" look. And we were both thinking prostitution, gambling, and opium, which would figure, because the Chinese took a blood oath of non-fraternization when they came to the Golden Mountain.

No fooling around with foreign devil-women, no drinking any kind of alcohol, no going into foreign bars, foreign restaurants, or foreign taverns. No gambling in the foreign devil gaming establishments.

As if the foreign devils would ever allow that to happen.

The ghosts of Buena Vista are: Helen, who haunts the tasting room, and she is a control freak; Chief Solano, who haunts along the old creek, and he is a guardian archetype; and the souls of the 19 Chinese workers who were buried alive in the big tunnel collapse.

I used to give tours at Buena Vista when the oldest building with the really deep tunnels was still open to the public. I know where the secret crossover tunnel is, and when part of my group wasn't looking, I would take a few guests back there, and we'd giggle while their friends tried unsuccessfully to figure out how we'd disappeared so completely. We'd reappear magically in the other tunnel, and laugh, and laugh.

I kissed my childhood sweetheart, Mike Deenihan, in that tunnel for the very first time. Mike Deenihan. Love at first sight. We married in 1978.

When they told us we had to call the coolies "Chinese Railroad Engineers" I quit giving tours at Buena Vista Winery. My mind had an off-color metaphor it wanted me to suggest to them, but I refrained, and instead I said:

"Why not call them International Transcontinental Railroad Engineers of the Asian American Buddhist Persuasion?"

People say it isn't true, but it is true that Count Haraszthy and General Vallejo dined off English china, and white linen, and ate a picnic lunch with silver forks and spoons, and listened to the screams of the trapped men. It is also true that they drank fine wine from crystal glasses, and smoked fancy Cuban cigars afterwards. But let me give these truths their due perspective.

When you own a vineyard, and you don't come home for supper because there is a life and death emergency at the winery, someone has to bring your food out to you. They didn't have Tupperware in those days, and they didn't have coolers, or Handy Wipes. When you sent food out to your boss, you put it in a basket, usually wicker, and to protect the contents you wrapped them in real linen, because real linen was what you had to work with.

Plastic had not yet been invented, so there were no plastic picnic forks, or paper cups, or Styrofoam plates. You used what you had, and that was real china plates, with real forks, real knives, real spoons, and usually in a rich man's house these utensils were made out of silver.

As for drinking fine wine from crystal glasses, yes, they did that. Mass production of cheap wine glasses had not yet been exported to Taiwan and China, so they used what they had, expensive crystal. The kind that requires padding, preferably with some fabric that could do double duty as a worthy serviette. Linen napkins, for example.

And again, this did happen at a winery, and that's what they made there, fine wine, so that was what was readily available to drink at a moment's notice. The wine they drank on this unhappy occasion probably hadn't even seen the inside of a bottle yet.

Sonomans drink unbottled wine all the time. Nowadays we call it "hose wine". Sonomans have even used wine to put out fires. So it's wasn't as though they were popping Champagne corks, and laughing their heads off over the imminent deaths of 19 lost Chinese souls, like drunk Roman's at a Bacchanal singing "Light Up A Few More Christians."

They were quite sober, I assure you.

What was sobering to them was not the 19 Chinese valued at 13 dollars apiece; that only tots up to $247.00. But over 300 casks of brandy buried with them at $25.00 a barrel tots up to $7,500.00. Let me spell that out to give it the respect it deserves: Seven thousand and five hundred dollars. That is quite a sum of money. Add that to the original investment of $247.00 and you have a grand loss of $7,747, which is almost $8,000. That's more than $80,000.00 worth of buying power in today's dollars. That is a sobering amount of money. That is an amount of money worth taking some time to think about. That might actually be an amount worth digging out.

Agoston Haraszthy and Guadalupe Vallejo needed those cigars.

It is possible that the Chinese in the cave-in actually survived. They were digging at the time of the cave-in; their tools were with them; they knew the placement of miles of other tunnels in the hillside about which the Occidentals knew absolutely nothing. If they got out in secret, they would have been assumed dead, and their contracts would be null and void. They would be free men. It is possible. The Buena Vista tunnel they were trapped in had secretly been dug out all the way into Napa County. There was even an exit up in Lovall Valley.

Thinking back, I have never heard of any first hand accounts involving Chinese ghosts at Buena Vista. I have been there when Kate Kennedy's summer Shakespeare Company had strange trouble with the wiring, and the electric lights, and the electronic equipment. I have been there when other people got the heebie-jeebies in the old stone winery's caves.

There is an unnaturally cold draft that sometimes comes out of the tunnels, but the reasonable explanation is that it's a natural convection current. So I'm not weighing in on the Chinese ghosts of Buena Vista yet. Not until I get over there with a professional, someone who has more than just my inadvertent psychic twinkle.

My only bad experience at Buena Vista was while Much Ado About Nothing was underway for the summer of 1990. There is no stage there, so we used the picnic area in front of the old winery building.

The green ivy is so thick you can't even see the light through the long narrow rifle slits designed for shooting Indians. And it's two stories high, so it makes a great natural backdrop.

We'd haul the picnic tables over, and set the plays in the round, with the Italian stone fountain as the centerpiece. People brought tablecloths and picnic dinner, and sometimes even silver candelabras, and the actors interacted with the audience. Sometimes the actors even ate their chicken. Talk about starving artists!

In the theatre world there are so many flakes, nuts, and space shuttles that if you show up when you say you will show up, and do what you say you will do, then you are well on your way to becoming a marvelous success.

The theater community is so small, word about you will get around fast, and pretty soon the phone will ring, and it will be someone you remember only vaguely calling from a party at Francis Ford Coppola's house to say that their stage manager flaked, and can you come over, and run things backstage for Dudley Moore at the Lincoln Theatre for the Napa Film Festival.

Here's the unbelievable part: They will even pay you. Don't laugh. This happened to me.

The only problem with using the flake-factor to get ahead is that it cuts both ways. If you do not show up when you say you will show up, and if you do not do what you say you will do, that gets around just as quickly, and you are anathema.

Damned for life.

Or at least until the current generation of directors dies off.

It is like living in a big family, or a small town, like Sonoma, where, once dirtied, your petticoat remains forever suspect.

So, with extreme anxiety born of dire necessity I borrowed six battery-operated custom made handheld lanterns for Much Ado About Nothing from Sonoma Ballet Conservatory director, Beth Marie Deenihan, on behalf of the Shakespeare company director, Kate Kennedy.

It was an arrangement upon which hinged my personal reputation.

In defense of flaky space shuttles everywhere, and in theatres the world over; please remember that theater is a place where anything that can go wrong does go wrong. How any production of anything ever comes together at all is, as the author of "Shakespeare In Love" said, a Mystery. In the miracle category, it's up there with transubstantiation.

Things going wrong in theatre isn't the exception that prove the rule. It's more like gravity. It's a Law.

Naturally, on the night we closed everybody vanished into the vineyards, and even the hard core inner circle had disappeared, and I'm back at home in my little bed at my little guest cottage in Buena Vista that used to belong to Ruth DeYoung Prosser, and just as I turn out the light, an unwelcome and unfinished piece of information hits me.

Twelve weeks ago I, Carla Heine, borrowed a set of six battery-operated custom made handheld lanterns for the night scene in Much

Ado from the Sonoma Ballet Conservatory director Beth Marie Deenihan on behalf of the Shakespeare company director Kate Kennedy.

The winery is all locked up, and I don't have a key, and my personal reputation will unhinge completely, and finally, if I don't get up out of my warm bed and go get those lanterns right now. It's after midnight. No moon. No keys to even get into the parking lot, and no flashlight because I think I know the place so well who needs a flashlight? Right?

Vanity. Thy name is Carla Heine.

So up I get, and out I go, and I haul my chubby round bottom over the top of the unexpectedly sharp spikes on the double-locked gate at the entrance to Buena Vista Winery. The parking lot is completely empty now, and it's a lot bigger than I remember it being, but ok. Fine. It's white gravel, and easy to negotiate, but just as my confidence swells up, I hit the dip that goes down into the dense woods that run along the old creek.

Suddenly everything goes jet black. Seriously, I've owned opal mines where you can't see your hand in front of your face that weren't as dark as that narrow one lane road along the creek down to Buena Vista Winery.

Halfway down I start to hear this crackle, crackle, snap. A sound of heavy walking on leaves and dry twigs, just off to my right. So I stop. I stop, and I hold stock-still. And the sound stops, too.

And I think, 'Where the Hell is my night vision? I used to have eyes like a cat!' But I still can't see my own tennis shoes.

And it's silent. Silent. Silent. No crickets. No bats. And there are always bats. Fruit bats love grapes. Nope. No bats.

No nothing!

Now, in the day-to-day course of normal events, I hear ultrahigh frequencies of sound, and I see ultrahigh frequencies of light, but there was nothing out there. Really nothing. Nothing living, anyway.

Dead silence.

Three minutes go by, because if you are going to use the start and stop method, you have got to give equal time to both the start, and the stop, or it won't work. Three minutes pass. Still nothing.

Nothing. Only the sound of my heartbeat.

'Remember when we were in fifth grade?' half my mind asks while the other half is going 'One hundred and forty-two, Mississippi; one hundred and forty-three, Mississippi.'

'I remember fifth grade.' I answer.

'Do you remember how you scared yourself silly on the walk home from school the winter Elizabeth got you those green corduroy pants?'

'I remember those pants.' Only one of the most humiliating experiences of my young life. Of course, I remember that, you idiot, I think frantically to myself.

'I remember that.' I say calmly to my mind. 'Thank you for sharing.'

It pays to be polite to voices like this under circumstances like these; you never know who you are talking to; someone with half a mind on Mississippi isn't all there from the get go.

'It took you three months, Carla, to figure out the noise that was following you home all winter was the swish, swish, swish of your corduroy pants as your thighs rubbed together.'

'Never mind my thighs.' I said curtly. 'What is your…'

'One hundred and fifty-five, Mississippi' says my mind helpfully.

'…point?'

'This is like that.' my mind says cheerfully, and adds, 'One hundred and fifty-six,, Mississippi.'

'No.' I say impatiently. 'This is not like that. I am wearing jeans.'

'Oh.' says my mind, and shuts up.

At one hundred and eighty Mississippi, having heard nothing from the dark, I began to walk firmly, but gently, and now I'm in charge of the count.

"One Mississippi. Two Mississippi. Three Mississippi." And at "Four Mississippi" the rustle-crack-snap begin to match me again. Step for step. All the way to "One hundred and eighty Mississippi".

And that's my signal to stop again, hold stock-still, and listen with all six senses.

"One Mississippi." And again: nothing. No rustle. No crickets. No high-pitched bat-squeaks. No glowing eyes, either. Now, there's a blessing.

It took four sets of 240 Mississippis to get to the front of the stone building where the lanterns were. The crackle of leaves, and the snap-crackle-snap of twigs followed beside me in the woods, less than six feet away.

My heavy-footed partner never missed a step.

He, she, or whatever it was, stopped when I got to the tasting room, and waited there.

The huge bronze Chinese bell that Ho Po the overseer for Buena Vista used to call the workers to and from the winery was invisible in the dark.

My sense of danger was brutal, but it lifted as I approached the big double doors of the original stone winery building. The black stage lanterns were right where they were supposed to be.

No box to put the lanterns in, but picking them up, counting them, and getting a grip on them gave me both something to think about, and something to hold onto.

Things were normal going back past the restrooms, normal past the tasting room, but the footsteps from the woods picked up again, right where they had left off, and matched me again, step by snap-snap step.

This time I didn't stop to test it.

Every step of the way my sense of danger deepened. Step for step with the crackle of leaves and the snap of twigs, there to my left the dark woods that run alongside the road became more and more menacing, and more and more threatening. Was this fear my own, reflected back at me to show me how wild and unsafe these deep woods really are?

At that point I left the woods, and came out of the dark onto the pale gravel. That was when I began to hurry. It was much better than being in the woods. May I have a big 'Amen?' 'Amen!' But I felt more afraid than ever.

The end was in sight.

Yes. But.

Have you ever noticed how fast things fall apart just when you think you are out of the woods?

Luckily, the lanterns all had these handy little loops of leather arched over their square tops, so when it came to breaking out of Buena Vista, it wasn't necessary for me to carry them with me over the sharp gate spikes. Whoever made these lanterns will never know how grateful I was for their attention to detail and craftsmanship. All I had to do was hang them along the outside of the gate on the lower spikes.

Up over the wrought iron gate went my body, and my soul was still intact, and the gate stood tall and strong between me and that silent partner back there in the dark.

It wasn't until I got back into bed, turned out the lights, and rolled over to go to sleep, that I realized every single one of those stage lanterns worked perfectly; as well as, if not better than, flashlights.

It was just as well I didn't use the lanterns in the dark woods. They would have blinded me. And what if that thing at my side was something normal like a bear, or a mountain lion? It would have seen how fat and meaty I was.

Was the danger I sensed so strongly in that black, blacker, blackest dark merely the danger inherent in any deep dark wood just twenty feet from the predatory untamed wild?

The danger of mountain lions in Sonoma is very real, and many a big brown bear has come down to Buena Vista Winery to see if some satisfied Shakespeare enthusiast misplaced a roast chicken.

Once I saw a Buena Vista bear lift the top off a dumpster with just one paw. He was tossing aside empty wine bottles like a real pro. Some Sonoma bears have developed an insatiable taste for Elaine Bell's honey roasted merlot and mustard barbeque sauce.

It was more than my sense of danger that followed me step for step, for a solid, very solid, stone cold solid, forty minutes that night. The right word for the overall sensation that remains with me from that night is terror. But thanks to the Smiling Man, I don't scare easily, and terror is rarer.

Something, or someone walked beside me and watched me from the woods that night. Watched me, yes, and I was terrified. My guardian angel was nowhere in evidence. That's scary, in and of itself.

I've been in trouble before. Who hasn't? I've been in life and death trouble. When your guardian angel's there, you have a sense of trust; not glee, not smugness, but trust. And a sense of security, and faith in the presence of danger and fear.

There was no security that night, unless that unseen presence was the spirit of Sum Yet Ho, Chief Solano, the Guardian Indian himself, and I was simply too scared to recognize him. And if it was he, why let me get so scared? He's supposed to comfort people.

My fear was appropriate. I was in over my head and I knew it. And sometimes fear is what we need to feel, to learn. Sometimes fear is a gift.

The Cedar Mansion

It would be hard for anyone raised as I was raised to live in something called The Cedar, or any other tree for that matter, Mansion. I would have to change the name.

According to Emily Post, and Elizabeth, my mother, one doesn't say "mansion"; one says "big house". One doesn't say "curtains"; one says "drapes". One doesn't say "geek"; one says "genius". And one doesn't say "brat" or "bastard"; one says "The Dad's not in the picture".

Cornel Gerdau's house is across the street from the Duhring House. At the moment it is called by the name the unwelcome and unsuccessful bed and breakfast people gave it: Cedar Mansion.

Fine.

Whatever.

It is a lovely house, by day, and by night, in sunlight, and in shadow. It's a true Victorian ship's captain's house. Nowadays, it's especially lovely because the family who lives there has children, and they celebrate Christmas, and Fourth of July, and Halloween with twinkie lights, and red, white, and blue bunting, and flags, and big orange pumpkins with carved faces that glow invitingly for Trick or Treaters from three counties.

There are no ghost stories here; only one tired old skeleton in the closet.

The Gerdau House has thick plush lawns, and old rose bushes, three darling boys, a mother who is a mother, and a father who is a father. It is what the Bible calls a "house in order" as opposed to what the Good Book calls "wide house" where anything goes.

The downstairs has a tall door that leads to a narrow stairway, which climbs with a purpose straight up to the roof and lets out directly onto the widow's walk. No windows. No handrails. Nor do the stairs stop on the second floor. No intermediary fainting room halfway to the top.

Colonel Gerdau's mother watched for Captain Gerdau's yellow silk flag fly off the mainmast of his ship down at the Embarcadero de Sonoma, and when she saw it as she stood on the top of their house, she sent the wagon, and the horse-drawn carriage to bring him home.

Each ship's captain's house in Sonoma had a flag like that. The lady of the house made it for her husband. Each house had a different color, so all the wives could watch from the top of their houses, and see when their husband came into port and home from the sea. Then they would send the carriage and a wagon down to fetch him home. Real Ladies never went "down there".

Captain and Mrs. Gerdau had two sons, Stanley, the eldest, and the Colonel, the youngest. Captain Gerdau was a merchant, so he wanted Stanley to go to sea with the Navy. Instead, Stanley joined the Merchant Marines, and saw the world and the war from that perspective. Stanley did his part in WWII.

The Colonel joined the Navy like his daddy wanted him to, so Captain Gerdau wrote Stanley completely out of his will, and left the house, the grounds, and everything he owned to his youngest son, the Colonel.

This sounds unfair to the modern mind, but in those days everything usually went to the eldest son, and an either-or mentality was significantly more common than a both-and mentality. It still is.

Unfortunately.

The Colonel inherited everything after the Captain died. And thus endowed the Colonel went everywhere in grand style, surrounded by an entourage of gorgeous bright young men in uniform, and out of uniform.

In Spring, in Summer, and in Autumn, Colonel Gerdau drove a long plump cream colored convertible Packard up and down Sonoma with the top down.

Whenever the Colonel drove by along Second Street, I heard champagne bubbles, and the twinkle of ice in crystal glasses. Laughter sparkled like fireworks, and delight followed the Packard up and down Sonoma's streets like pixie dust from Neverland. The skeleton in the Gerdau family closet was gay as Dad's old hatband.

Stanley lived quietly in the carriage house in front of the little dock by the boathouse behind the big house. He worked regularly at the Biggs' place, which is now Macarthur Place.

Stanley walked out the gate every weekday morning at dawn with his coffee mug full of whiskey, and his curly handlebar moustache neatly waxed.

He came home every evening at sunset, with his coffee cup full of whiskey, and the coat-tails of his long charcoal duster flapped like ravens' wings in the evening breeze.

The hat Stanley wore was a round pillbox hat, not slouched like a cavalry bummer, but neatly squared off, like half of a one-pound coffee can, covered in dark blue wool with a thin band of gold braid for decoration.

Stanley's skin was pink, his hair was black and gray, and his eyes were Harold Burrell blue, oystering into red.

Stanley's side of Second Street was the West side of Second Street, and if you went anywhere along Second Street, it was best to stay on the East side of the street, and give Stanley a wide berth.

Not that he had ever hurt anybody.

But Stanley had been "away" and that, in and of itself, made Stanley an unknowable quantity to Sonoma proper.

Stanley had served his country during the second World War, that was a fact, and here in Sonoma, people respect a Veteran, so long as they don't rub your nose in it, but Stanley had been in exotic foriegn ports, and seen and probably even done exotic foriegn things.

It did not pay to take chances. Oh no!

Stanley was really very charming once you got to know him. He was not bitter. He was not rude, or forward. He was just Stanley. Like Robert the Vampire turned out to be just Robert. Stanley did odd jobs now and then, and kept himself on an even keel. Which is more that most people can say for themselves. It isn't easy to do, even under the best of circumstances.

When Beth Marie and I were older, from our early twenties and into our late thirties, Stanley left roses and daisies on the windshields of our cars for us. Just like Robert the Vampire would leave pastries and almond cookies on our porches and back steps from time to time. Till the day Stanley and Robert disappeared.

I loved Stanley, and his ready smile, and his old Sonoma stories. He was a big part of my life, very present in my childhood fears, and ever-present in my grown-up day-to-day life.

Then suddenly, one gray, winter soaked afternoon, Stanley was gone.

No obituary. No funeral. No memorial service. No conversation. No explanation. Nothing. Just, no Stanley.

Exactly like when Eddie died. Zip. Nada. Silencio. An unfillable void.

People still see Stanley from time to time at sunrise as he walks to work, and at sunset, as he walks back from work. Always on the West side of Second Street. Always flapping along the sidewalk in his long black duster, with his coffee mug full of whiskey, and his pillbox hat.

When you walk down Second Street East at sunset, and you see a tall, thin, mustachioed man with a mug and a long black Dr. Wango Tango duster, don't worry.

It's only Stanley, the Second Street ghost.

Deuce A L'Orange

At the corner of Broadway and Andrieux Street is a lemon cream building with a sculpted topiary hedge that says, in dark green leafy bushes on a funerary mound of richly fertilized greenery, "Deuce".

Deuce is the name of the two of hearts, the card of friendship, of healing friendship in the Tarot deck, and by proxy in the regular Bicycle deck of cards. In poker it means a pair. In prison lingo, it means a two-year sentence, or a petty thief who is so small-time he never gets paid more than two dollars, or sentenced to more than two years. It is also a euphemism for the Devil.

Archaic as it is, it still crops up occasionally in films and literature in the expressions "The Deuce, you say!" and "To the Deuce with you!" This word was formerly taboo because it was an oath; a swearword and a curse all at the same time.

In the language of the modern restaurant entrepreneur, a deuce is a table for two.

The best table for two at Deuce restaurant in Sonoma is the outdoor balcony table, halfway down the wall to your left as you stand at the hostess's station with your back to the bar. It has tall arched wing doors, and a location that affords you superb views of the gardens as well as the interiors of the restaurant. The staff keeps an extra eye out for you without intruding, because it is the most romantic table in the house, and they want you to have a perfect experience. The same man who did the large gate in front of the garden that faces Broadway, and the railing on the front steps did the wrought iron work on this balcony. The theme is curves, curls, and vines. There was a black wrought iron gargoyle on the gate by the same artist, but either Harry Marsden took it with him when he left, or someone stole it.

"Where should we put the kitchen?" Ed asked me as we studied the wide roll of pale blueprints. They were off-white with thin cornflower blue lines and notations. The outer edges of the sheets were dry, chipped, and jaundiced. They were a far cry from the endless rolls of thick bright royal blue sheets Ed used to home from the office for Eddie and me when we were little.

Those blueprints were sapphire blue. They had the clean white lines of Ed's designs, and his neat square printing on the front, and a limitless amount of empty space on the back. Blue and white rolls of blueprints punctuated my childhood with each new job Ed completed.

"Why are our Christmas presents always wrapped in Ed's blueprint paper?" I asked Elizabeth.

"Santa has to use something." she said in an 'isn't that obvious' tone.

68

For Eddie and for me, Ed's blueprints were our Samurai warrior hats, our afternoon kites, our giant origami toys, and an endless supply of wide-open adventure for crayons, colored pencils, and watercolors.

I feel sorry for kids who are stuck with little postage stamps of eight and a half by eleven printer paper. So should you. There isn't a piece of paper in the world big enough to express half the artistic inspiration in one four year old with a broken crayon.

Eddie and I were lucky to have Ed's unlimited supply of old blueprint paper.

It wasn't that Ed was such a great and famous architect, but he was a busy architect. And he made little working models of every building he designed, and he let me play gently with them through long rainy afternoons on the rough gray Berber carpet of his office floor.

He made all our best toys himself. And Ed had smelly colored felt pens before regular felt pens were available to regular people. He gave us all of the ones that were starting to wear out. His office was at 3030 Bridgeway in Sausalito. Ed did that building, too, in exchange for free rent, and the best office with the best light.

He was chief architect for Holiday Inn, and Howard Johnson's, which is like a Carrow's franchise.

Ed designed the Pizza Hut prototype, with the funny red hat, and the Taco-Bell prototype with it's arched South-of-the-border walls. He designed the original Trans-America building in San Francisco when it was the highest skyscraper on the skyline.

Ed was chief architect for Kingston Trio Properties, and Frank Werber, the man who owned Capital Records and Columbia Records, as well as the Trident Restaurant in Sausalito. Frank had SS numbers tattooed on his wrist.

My father also designed a lot of big winter ski-lodges up at Squaw Valley near Lake Tahoe, and he made deals with their owners, so we could use them every winter. We skied. Ed was a downhill slalom racer on the US team in the European Olympics. We skied.

His tarnished silver medal rests peacefully in my Venetian jewelry casket.

We might come home to a house where the electricity and telephone was turned off for non-payment, and to an empty refrigerator, but there was always money for new cars, and a month or two of skiing every year.

Ed designed the Ondine and the Tradewinds restaurants in Sausalito.

Oh, and a big private hunting lodge at Covelo, where the US Cavalry isolated 20,000 Indians from many different tribes in the 1860's. It took 8 weeks them to die. Round Valley is Mendocino County's equivalent of Sonoma's Lovall Valley. It is often called the California Holocaust.

We flew up there a lot for that job. Ed kept the family plane at Sky Park down on Eight Street East. It was a thrill to fly in to Covelo, because Covelo has the shortest runway in the whole United States.

The same team of craftsmen who did the woodwork for the original Trident restaurant came in for the fabulouso Au Relais, which became the eh-so-so-ugh Magulio's, which became the marvelouso Deuce.

All through the Spring of 1972 I was persona non-gratis with Ed and Elizabeth. In an effort not to set him off with the wrong answer, when Ed asked me where the kitchen should go, I ducked the question.

With Ed I was persona non-grata, for coming back home to be a burden on the family halfway through school, and for not staying far away in Boulder and working my way through my BS degree, and my MD.

With Elizabeth I was persona non grata for dropping out of the best Greek house in the system, Kappa Alpha Theta, for dropping out of college without either a degree, or a rich husband, and for making her look bad in public to an audience of invisible people I neither knew, nor met, nor cared to meet.

"Nobody ever helped me through college." Ed complained.

But Ed had the GI Bill. That helped him get his degree in architecture at University of Chicago. And he got an advanced degree in engineering from University of Munich in 1941, shortly before they started pulling all the Jewish professors out onto the streets and shoving them into cattle cars.

Only three years earlier, the American publication, Time Magazine, named Hitler "Man of the Year". In 1940 Time named Stalin "Man of the Year".

There's no accounting for taste.

Hitler and his friends liked to go to Tegernsee outside Munich in the Bavarian Alps, and enjoy nature. One time, while he was visiting at my grandparents' country place above the lake, Hitler asked the family if he could buy it. How rude is that, for a guest to ask such a question of his host? Like, that's a nice gold watch you're wearing. May I buy it?

He was told no, but that he could have the blueprints, and the blueprints formed the basis for his country place, which he built in Prussia (talk about class-envy) and named "Wolf's Lair". "Wolf-Lager" in German. The name looses much of its menace and wildness in the translation to English.

"How could anyone say 'No' to Hitler?" I asked Ed. He told me.

"Hitler had a peasant's awe for the aristocracy. He admired our family because of its background, but he hated us for it, too. He felt lucky to know them socially. He wasn't their social equal. But he couldn't resist them."

Thanks to Ed's attendance at private semi-secret anti-Nazi meetings in Munich, Ed met the man who would fly him out of Germany. He was a

WWI flying ace, and a German folk hero who had received the Blue Max. He became Ed's political mentor.

The SS hated this guy, but they cut him a lot of slack because he had been such a popular war hero, and they could not persecute him, for fear of alienating the common men and women who idolized him.

The year was 1941. Ed was 19. The United States was about to get off its non-involvement policy, and finally enter the "war to end all wars". Ed escaped from Nazi Germany to America with this man and his son, who was a college classmate at the University in Munich. They took his private plane. Ed's mother, Johanna Koester Heine, and his two younger half-brothers, Robert and Peter, went with them, abandoning the family's houses in Cologne, and Munich, and the house in Tegernsee, and two car factories they owned on what would become the other side of the Berlin Wall.

For the SS it was not so much an escape as it was a good way to remove an inconveniently outspoken, and revered hero of the Fatherland who refused to join the Nazi Party. Letting him "escape" got rid of him without upsetting the status quo, such as it was. It afforded the SS a convenient viable means to discredit him and his dangerous, traitorous political ideas, and ideals.

There is little doubt in my mind that other members of our family were working from within the Nazi Party to derail Hitler when the perfect time and the perfect opportunity presented itself. Given the number of relatives who were arrested after the July 20th assassination attempt, it's a certitude.

There would have been no escape for my father and his mother and brothers, if their attempt had not been made before Johanna's cousin, a man with one leg, one arm, and one eye, put a bomb under Hitler's table. If they had not waited so long, if he had done it when he got the news of the American commitment to become involved in WWII, I might never have been born. How many parallel universes exist where he succeeded?

When you think about it, if they had not waited, and if they had acted and succeeded in 1941, the entire gene pool of the world would have been impacted. For better, or for worse.

Hollywood made a movie about Cousin Claus. The release had to be delayed until after the 2008 presidential elections. The timing was bad. It came out on Christmas Day. Predictibly enough they ignored a main point. He was against the strong centeralized government and wanted to restore local self-government and basic Constitutional rights. Maybe that is what made the film unsuitable for the national election of 2008.

The SS caught them on the way to the airport, and Ed had to go to Auschwitz to meet the SS officers, and promise to carry microfilm to Detroit for them in an Edgar Allen Poe paperback book; "The Gold Bug".

What the SS knew, which Edmund did not know, was that his legal father had been one of their spies for some time. What's more, he and Johanna had no idea that Hitler would not win the war; until the news reached them that the Americans would be entering the fight.

Once America got off the fence, it was "Auf vieder sehen!"

When Ed got to Detroit, to his father's house, he put "The Gold Bug" on a shelf in Edmund Senior's library. A few weeks later, on his way home from a date at the movies, he saw armed FBI and CIA men surrounded the house.

They arrested Edmund Carl Heine, Senior, that night, along with the rest of the Dungeness Spy Ring. On January 2, 1942, 33 members of

74

the Nazi spy ring headed by Frederick Joubert Duquesne were sentenced to serve a total of over 300 years in prison.

My father kept his mouth shut about the Gold Bug microfilm, but they walked right in and pulled it off the shelf. Ed said he thought it was all a misunderstanding, and that his dad would turn out to be innocent of all the charges, but he wasn't. He had been sending airplane engine designs and other blueprints to other Nazis back in Germany as his part of the war effort.

He even sent them the plans for the rotary engine.

Even though Ed's legal father was sentenced to five years in prison, Edmund Senior only did a deuce; two years. Henry Ford owned a number of Senators, and he always looked out for the men who gave his illegitimate children legitimacy by wedding his pregnant personal secretaries.

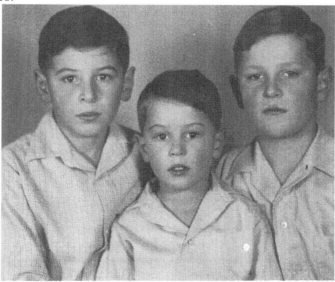

After the arrest, Mr. Ford gave Johanna, my grandmother, and the boys a bigger, better house, and he hired Ed to work on soybean research in his laboratory, so they would have some money coming in while Ed Senior was in prison, and so their having any money at all would not look funny, and upset Mrs. Ford.

So Ed had financial help for college from his legal father, and from his biological father, and from the Army. I applied for help, but Ed made too much money to qualify for scholarships. I was sixteen when I graduated from Sonoma Valley Union High School, and Ed refused to emancipate me so I could apply for college loans on my own. No blame. It all worked out.

"Use your brain, Carla." Ed said, as we looked at the yellowed blueprints of the building that would someday become Deuce. Ed was always my teacher, uber alles. "What does a commercial kitchen need?"

"I don't know." I said, touchy from being the family scapegoat since I came home from college at Christmas in a wheelchair. Even my skin felt thin. Malnutrition had taken its toll. I was naive enough to think a person could live on a one hundred pound bag of brown rice for a semester, and tutor French, and Calculus, and carry 25 pre-med units at the same time through the Rocky Mountain winter.

"Well, first of all, you are going to need light." Ed said. "Which room has the most power outlets for light fixtures?"

Why was he bothering with me at all? It wasn't like he wanted me to enter the family business. All he and Elizabeth felt I was fit for now was marriage, preferably to the highest bidder. I wondered how things might have gone if Len Dillman had been filtyh rich, and not a soda jerk from over there on Riverside Drive in El Verano.

"OK." I said. I took a breath in, and looked at the layout on the gray and yellow prints. "You need light. You need water. You'll need plenty

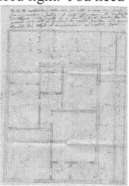

of electricity, and you'll need drainage for the big kitchen sinks."

"And which room has all four?" Ed prompted.

"This room." I pointed at the correct room with the tip of my mechanical pencil.

"Right." says Ed, pleased with himself for finally getting through to me. "The slab room."

It isn't everyone who can convert a small town mortuary into a viable restaurant, but when the building was finished, the task of making it work as a restaurant fell entirely into the hands of Harry and Max.

"People don't care how far they have to drive. If the food is good, they will find you." Harry Marsden said. And Max certainly proved that at Au Relais, and with his own restaurant, The Kenwood.

Maxim's food is to die for.

Harry and Max studied Cordon Bleu cooking in Paris. Where else?

They lived in a house of blue lights near the Place Pigalle, and they made a deal with the Madame for room and board. In exchange they did all the cooking.

This worked out really well, but as they became more and more expert at their craft, people started to forget about visiting the girls, and began to come in just for the food.

Eventually Harry and Max had to move out.

Success with the Au Relais in the early Seventy's definitely went to Harry's head. He started acting like he owned the palace, which he did, with Dorothy his wife, and with Max his partner, but even Max didn't act like he owned the palace.Harry acted like he owned us.

He became the archetypical incarnation of Henry the Eighth.

Nothing exceeds like excess.

When Harry finally realized that it was not working, he went into rehab at the clinic in Saint Helena. But he couldn't stand the menu. So he took over the kitchen, and soon visitors were staying on for dinner, and by the time Harry was cured, people were going there just for the food.

Harry Marsden came to say good-bye to me shortly after he died on September 15th, 1992, at the age of 52. He had two pretty young lovelies hanging off each arm. They dangled on his ever glance, and word. He was wearing Henry the Eighth's signature portrait costume. He looked about 36.

"You should live it up a little," Harry told me, "or you will hardly have lived at all before you die."

He never understood why I didn't have children.

King Hal.

"You work at Deuce now, right?" I asked my next-door neighbor as we stood between my limousine and her hot, red-hot, Camero.

"Yes." she said. "I work there now."

"Do you like it?" I asked.

"Yes. They're nice people. I like it."

"Have you ever experienced anything unusual there? Anything fantastical?"

"Yes." she said. "Now that you mention it, I saw a tray of wine glasses slide off the waitress station all by itself, and they all crashed down onto the floor. Nobody touched it. It just flew out, and then, crashed down."

"Was it the station near the swinging doors to the kitchen?" I asked.
 "Yes." She said eyes wide and mouth in an O. "How did you know that?"

"I was the first hostess there, when it opened as the Au Relais. I saw the exact same thing happen."

Harry Marsden swung through doors from the kitchen and saw the shattered wineglasses on his new parquet floor.

"What the Hell are you doing, Carla?" he yelled in his Manchester street accent. Harry's accent got worse when he was upset. You could tell from the moment he opened his mouth that he grew up in an industrial row house.

It was the second week after the Au Relais opened, and Harry was mad at everybody. A dozen broken glasses were the last straw at the end of a bad day. "Do you have any idea how much money I have sunk into this place? I can't afford to have people go around breaking the Goddamn wineglasses! Jesus Christ, Carla!"
I burst into tears.

Not only had I been a part of Harry's bad day, but Max was mad at me, too. And back at the house, Elizabeth was twisting the thumbscrews to make me go out with John Rothschild on the theory that my only asset was my ass.

That very morning, when Ed dropped me off at the Au Relais, he had actually begged me to go out with John Rothschild. Ugh!

"Just for awhile, Carla. Just to get Elizabeth off my back." Ed pleaded. "You don't know how mean she can be when she doesn't get her way." He was wrong about that. They had both elevated "mean" to the level of an art form.

"If she likes him so much, why doesn't she go out with him?" I asked.

Ed laughed out loud. That took the edge off. Then he sobers up, and says ruefully, "She's driving me out of my mind." I felt exactly the same way. I'd felt that way before I left for Boulder in the Spring of 1970. Before Dr. Schafer diagnosed Eddie's Leukemia.

Elizabeth changed. After Eddie died she withdrew from all of us, poured three coats of quick-drying Verathane on top of her world-view and pronounced it complete. I blamed the house for making it worse than it had to be. The house was hungry. The house wanted more.

And there was more.

We fed its demons with our hateful fights over my grades, my major, my college, my clothes, my horse, my ass, my everything. Elizabeth was like a woman possessed of an unclean spirit, and a snot-green miasma emanated from that unclean house. I have to admit, she wasn't the only one infected.

"Leave the bitch." I said to Ed.

"I can't do that." Ed whined. "We have two school-aged children, Honey, I can't do that to her.

Now, here I was, on the other end of that same bad day, a dozen smashed wine glasses at my feet, and Harry Marsden, my first real employer, red as a beet, serious as a heart attack, and mad as Hell.

When chefs get mad they get really mad.

When short chefs get mad, throw away the key.

My sudden outburst of tears unmanned him. Harry Marsden switched gears like a schizophrenic on steroids. Harry Marsden actually apologized to me.

Harry Marsden actually forgave me right there on the spot.

Harry Marsden still owed Ed money.

Strange things happened at the Au Relais in that early Sonoma Spring and Summer. That's understandable, after the conversion of the building from a mortuary to a restaurant. Anton LeVey was in there all the time. The Au Relais was Anton LaVey's favorite restaurant. He told me so himself.

Anton Szandor LaVey was the author of The Satanic Bible, and high priest of The First Church of Satan, based out of San Francisco.

One balmy bright afternoon Anton LaVey pulled up in front of the Au Relais in a little red Alpha Romero. He wore a black leather driving cap that had a jaunty lilt to the brim. He bounced out of the car, and opened the passenger door for a vision of loveliness.

Five feet six in stiletto heels, voluptuous, pneumatic, and all woman.

All ideal woman. Big round innocent eyes, and long thick straight blonde on California blonde hair. She was to die for. This proud beauty had rosy cheeks, cataclysmic cleavage, and a smile hot enough to melt the Polar Icecaps.

However, from the porch outside the front doors, with my hands on the wrought iron railing of the good ship Au Relais, not all the loveliness in this world, or the next, could defuse my first impression of Anton LaVey.

"You look to me," I weighed the word with the risk in my mind, and said, "like a Pirate."

"I am." He grinned as he ascended the front steps. "I am a Pirate of Souls."

Later Harry Marsden told me who he was, and I raced home, raced back, and LaVey signed my first edition copy of his book for me. Then he told me I lived a charmed life. I sure hoped he was right, because right then, my life was the pits.

You may remember Anton LaVey's daughter. In 1972, when he introduced her to me, she looked about 16. The whole Church of Satan thing started out as a tongue in cheek joke, but it evolved into the real thing very quickly because there were those who took it so very seriously.

The LaVey's just played it along, rode into the roles, and played them out. Their satanic mystique brought them into the company of celebrities and other esoteric circles they would otherwise never have known socially.

The Hollywood glamour held both LaVey and his wife in certain awe. They hoped for advancement and recognition by relating as members of one power-aristocracy to another. Cough, cough. Sputter, sputter. As though!

The LaVey's began to associate with many famous and accomplished people, particularly actors, writers, and circus people from Anton's former life. There was Jayne Mansfield, Sammy Davis Jr., and Joseph Cotton who was never the same after starring in "Portrait of Jenny". They met and carried on with Barbara McNair, Elke Sommer, and even William Shatner.

As I recall his daughter sued him, for using a minor as a Satanic altar, and under the child abuse laws of California, she won an award of $6,000,000.00.

That year there were big orbs in the mortuary that became the Au Relais.

Not little dot orbs the size and color of oranges, like Off the Hook TV caught on the HPI (Haunted Paranormal Investigators, International) Eldridge video on You Tube, but big orbs like the ones that swoosh down the mountain in "Close Encounters of the Third Kind". The Au Relais orbs were a good three, and four feet across. And strong energy.

I had never seen orbs before, but I have seen them since. Mellow orbs like the ones at Irene Cunha's Art Farm at the corner of Fifth Street East and Macarthur, where she gives spiritual advice, cuts hair, and sells art, corn, corn doll angels, and harvest wreaths, veggies, sage, basil, and fine art paintings.

Many non-psychics see orbs out at Irene's Art Farm.

Sonomans who are from here go there to see Irene and buy her special sage.

Regular sage is worse than no good in Sonoma. We have three formal covens in Sonoma Valley, and they all use regular sage.

Unless you are one of their kind, Dear, go see Irene.

The orbs are the least of the phenomena at Irene Cunha's Art Farm. Once part of the inevitable Sonoma Spanish land grant, the land has strong Indian spirit energy, and it gets occasional crop circles, too. The well there is still fed by an original pre-1906 Earthquake spring springs, and there is a nice little winter creek behing the walnut orchard.

UFO's like water.

There is a small saucer-shaped UFO that has been landing for centuries on the Indian mound at West Spain and Second Street. There used to be a big spring there, and it was where the servants of the Chiefs and

Shamans made camp during the Bear Sacrifice. It was a midden, but it is all covered up with dirt now. Stand on top of it with your eyes shut, and you will get really, really dizzy. The light energy there literally pulls you around.

The Au Relais orbs were very active and agile, like the ones I saw in the dark on my motorcycle trip through the Superstition Mountains. They were bright white ones that took turns rolling by me with the careening ghosts of stagecoaches along the edges of a 3,000-foot drop into the steep black canyon.

On the Triple A map, the mountain range shows twenty miles of unimproved road, as the crow flies, and I entered the canyon 20 minutes before sunset on my Honda 400.

The sun didn't just go down; it slammed down. There is no twilight interval in deep canyons. But who knew that? The light went out like God Himself had flipped off the switch. It took two long dark hours on a road that had not been improved since 1850 to get from the only canyon entrance, up over the top of the mountain crest, and down again to the only canyon exit.

The silt was between six and twelve inches deep, and if my bike hadn't been going 125 when the rear tire blew 25 miles outside of El Paso the night before, and if she hadn't fishtailed like a bucking bronco as I took the new engine down through the gears, and if we hadn't ridden that wild ride out together, I'd have dumped that little Honda ten feet after I first hit the silt.

The motorcycle had to be walked almost half the time anyway. No street lights. No houses. No moon. Only the single headlamp on the Honda, the orbs, and the torches of raucous phantom stagecoaches flying past me, Hell bent for leather.

When I finally got out of the canyon, the first living creature I saw was a cow. I was so thrilled to see another living being that I waved frantically to the cow, and yelled "Hello! Hello!"

I caught myself and felt extremely silly.

The big orbs at the Au Relais came when the restaurant closed between lunch and dinner, when the whole staff was together in the kitchen.

Between lunch and dinner we girls sometimes went home to take an afternoon nap. Nanette, Amy, Suzanne, Michelle Latiolais, and me.

We'd go to whoever's house was quietest that day, kick off our shoes, take off most of our clothes, take the pins out of our hair, and lie down on the beds in the big rooms.

We wore white cotton camisoles and bloomers.

Admittedly, there was an erotic element to it. How could there not be, with all those hormones flying around the room?

But it was a passing flicker of occasional moments, and not the distinguishing characteristic of the situation.

Looking around the room before I dozed off, I realized that Harry and Max had hired beautiful girls. I was the eldest by three years, and I felt like an old maid by comparison, but these girls were exquisite. The full bloom of their youth and innocence blushed into the edges of glowing sensuality.

To see them stretched out like lazy kittens across the vast white linen spaces echoed back to a feeling I used to get at Sunday teas, and at times when the Children's Telegraph brought news to the house at 205.

It was a final transition that precedes the end of an era; a cultural tradition was disappearing right before my eyes; passing away, passing over, and not passing on to the next generation of Sonoma's girls and women. Like the nap before the barbeque that Scarlet O'Hara went to, where the girls undress to their undergarments and nap together in the sleepy afternoon heat, just before they find out that the first shot had been fired at Vicksburg, and the life they thought would last forever was over with, done for, and Gone With the Wind.

Sometimes we stayed at the restaurant during the afternoon break, and Harry made huge batches of spaghetti and meatballs. While he cooked, and the dishwashers cleaned up the last of the lunch dishes, and the sous-chefs tidied up the salad stations and prep-counters, we all drink ice water, or sodas, and everybody would talk.

The new kitchen was bright, modern, and cheerful; the exact opposite of how the old mortuary slab room looked. When we were all relaxed like that, everyone forgot its original condition, and its original purpose.

One orb was lush peachy pink. One was sky blue and opal swirls ebbing across the transparent silver surface. Another was plain red, and very energetic; and another was a coral orange with yellow highlights. One was a pure brilliant white almost too bright to look at straight on. I liked them all; except for the one that was snot-green.

As the conversation went around the big commercial kitchen, these orbs sprang from person to person. They hovered over the person who spoke, and each orb's color corresponded to the tone of the speaker. They hovered above us like huge beach balls seen from the bottom of the swimming pool, and then they took turns changing places as the conversation changed.

They never picked one person to spin over the whole time, but they changed partners, and switched off. It was a dance. If there was music, it would have been the music of the spheres, but I didn't hear anything except the bantering conversation of the staff.

When the topic was sexual, or lusty, or warlike, the red orb hovered over that speaker. When it was a fresh innocent comment, the peach orb moved in over the speaker. When it was intellectual, or informational, the light blue opal orb took a turn.

When they weren't hovering over a speaker, they simply bobbed above all of us, a few feet below the high ceiling. The orbs flew in to hover above the speaker a half-second before they spoke, but they waited until the speaker finished to zoom back up to the ceiling.

The snot-green orb's specialty was swearwords, unpleasant remarks, sarcasm, and belittling comments. It could have been worse.

These colorful orbs were a wonder to behold, and I could barely believe what I saw with my own eyes. The orbs moved beautifully in a playful and symphonic dance.

Later, I asked the others who were simpatico, and confirmed that we all saw the same thing. The dense people saw nothing, and Harry Marsden, Chef Extraordinaire, was busy with his eyes, and his hands, on the food.

Mother's Day is the busiest and most profitable day of the year in the restaurant business. It's like Easter for lapsed Catholics. People come pouring out of the woodwork to prove their love.

Or to prove something.

One Mother's Day Eve, after everything had been set up for the big Sunday ahead, the restaurant was locked up tight, and everyone had gone home. You try to get as much as possible done the night before every day, but that goes quadruple for Mother's Day.

Restaurants are live theatre, for those who know how to watch the show. And like live theatre, anything that can go wrong, will go wrong.

So you frantically, maniacally, insanely try to control what you can before the curtain goes up, then let go, and hope for the best.

At five in the morning on Sunday, Mother's Day, the head chef showed up to do the prep work that cannot be done the night before. He unlocks the back doors, comes in the back way, goes through the kitchen, swings through the swinging doors, walks up the isle along the wall with the tables for two, which used to be the coffin display area, and when he passes the hostess station, where the reservation book sits, he stops.

All the bottles of wine, hard alcohol, beer and liquor had been removed from the cabinets and shelves behind the bar. They all lay out on their sides, on the parquet floor. It was very neat and tidy, and would have taken some time to accomplish, but nobody had been in the building since it was locked up the night before.

Who created this 8 by 12 foot glass carpet of adult beverages?

The chef checked the locks on all the doors and windows, but there was no sign of entry, forced, or otherwise. Nor were there any signs of an intruder, who would surely have popped a beer, because it looked like thirsty work.

There were no signs of snacking either.

If it had been me, I would have made myself a sandwich.

The obvious explanation, which is sometimes the best explanation, was that this had not been done by anybody. Nobody had done it. Or somebody with no body.

The building originally belonged to an extremely pro-temperance family. They were actual members of Sonoma's Temperance League.

Unlike Mr. and Mrs. Steiner who said "Pish Posh" to Prohibition and kept pouring, the original owners of the house that is now Deuce forbid the use of alcohol for anything, except as a cleaning solvent for their mortuary tools.

The people who built the house that is now Deuce got into the mortician's trade, the "quiet trade" as it is called by those in the know, accidentally.

The father was a tinsmith who came from San Francisco. People in Sonoma who couldn't afford to bury their family members up on the hill in The Sonoma Mountain Cemetery, had to bury them down in Sonoma's flat land in the potters' field for Protestants and Chinese.

Before the morning of the 1906 earthquake, Sonoma was only three feet above sea level, and people who wanted a burial in the potters' field really needed a lined coffin. A waterproof lined coffin.

By the end of that afternoon nobody really needed waterproof coffins anymore. Sonoma was suddenly 84 feet above sea level, but it was too late; ordering a tin-lined coffin in Sonoma was a knee-jerk reaction.

They had been conditioned.

"These humans are so suggestible." I once overheard an alien say to a co-worker during a standard procedure. "Show them a few postcards, and they think they've been there."

In Sonoma people used to bring their coffins to the tin-smith for lining, but after awhile he expanded into coffin building, and his wife was handy with a needle, so she lined the coffins, and made ruffles, and as time went by they found themselves well situated in the quiet trade.

The big dining room with the picture window and the table for 12 at Deuce was their viewing room, where people paid final respects to their loved ones.

So it was, that the lined coffin came to be invented in Sonoma.

Have you ever asked yourself how one goes into the quiet trade?

One way is by accident. Another way is by entering the family business. It is often a generational profession, like becoming a doctor, or a sin-eater.

A few decades back, on a rabid hormone-driven hunt for a suitable mate, I met a nice man named Paul. Paul was "not from here". Paul was from "away".

"Away" is where everybody goes when they leave Sonoma.

Paul was from The Midwest.

Paul was handsome in an Oxford shirt and loafers way, but what got me about him, aside from his big blue Len Dillman eyes, was that his manners were so smooth, and Paul so invariably understood everything. He had an almost infinite level of compassion. You see it in saints and rabis, in gurus, and other great beings.

Paul was fastidious and clean, too. He smelled great, and he manicured his own nails. He was mature, responsible, and heterosexual. A good thing in a candidate for me. Paul was also a nice man. A really, really nice man.

"I wouldn't know a nice man if one walked up and hit me in the face." I had said at a CODA Twelve Step meeting a few weeks before I met Paul.

"Carla," said an old friend from Sonoma, with whom I had missed sleeping by a good six inches, "A nice man wouldn't walk up and hit you in the face."

"I rest my case." I said.

The kick-out factor with this nice man, Paul, turned out to be Paul's profession.

Paul was in the quiet trade.

Paul's company had just bought out the Bates, Evans, and Gail Feherensen's Mortuary. That business started in the house that is now Deuce. It moved to a modern building directly across from the high school.

Not that any of us at Sonoma High ever thought we'd get old, let alone die.

I used to wonder where all the old people in Sonoma came from. We all did. We never looked at Bate's Evans and Feherensen's; it was a Sonoma blind spot, like the old port down at the bottom of Broadway, or The Blue Wing Inn, or the wooden sidewalk where the boy in brown disappeared forever into the seventeen miles of Chinese tunnels under Sonoma.

Or like the silver wire of the rabbit-warren poetry in "Watership Down".

Paul told me that only 20% of Americans cremate their dead. The Discovery channel said that it was up to 25% in 2008. Paul also said that Mr. Feherensen had donated all the original funerary tools that had come from the house that now is Deuce to the Museum of Funerary Arts in Texas. Paul said that the museum was extremely grateful to have them for their collection, because nobody anywhere had tools that went back as far as those. Except, of course, the Egyptians.

I did like Paul's sense of humor.

As I said, we have three formal "covens" in Sonoma. Two are Satanic, and one is Luciferian. One coven is a cult that involves sex with five-year old children, and they are an understandably tight-lipped crowd.

We also have The Breakfast Club. These are parents who swap spouses for the night, and then all the family members have breakfast together the next morning. Each of these subculture groups has special terms and phrases; key words that transmit information without revealing anything to outsiders.

Have you ever heard a gay man ask if So-and-So "Knows Dorothy"?

That is a discreet way of asking, in heterosexual company, if So-and-So is gay. As in, "Toto, I don't think we're in Kansas anymore".

The group in Sonoma that interests me most at the moment is the group that meets with the Abraham channeler. It's a new group; they meet privately on Monday nights here in town; they post videos on You Tube. They call dying "croaking" because we put too much dread-energy around death, and they say "there is no death", but only "the transition" from this "life-form" to "the next".

In the quiet trade they have special terms, too. Like "braining and draining".

In America today we enjoy a certitude that often goes unacknowledged. Thanks to Russian spiritualist Madame Blavatsky, we can rest in peace.

Federal law requires that the human brain be removed from the cranial cavity and the blood be removed from the deceased before interment can legally occur. This law exists thanks to someone who channeled, not Abraham, but a departed human spirit named Mary.

Not Mary Bailey; just Mary, for now. I don't have her full name yet. Mary came through a medium who channeled spirits of the dead for a group of Theosophists. Mrs. Robert Johnson, who built and occupied the fireswept Castle below Castle Canyon, she was a Theosophist.

This did nothing to endear her to Sonoma proper.

The Theosophists follow the spiritual teachings of Madame Helena Petrova Blavatsky upon which many if not most of today's new age precepts are based. In accordance with the new "scientific method" of experimentation, this group of her followers kept scrupulous notes of every séance they conducted, as well as minutes from their meetings, and papers with automatic spirit writing. This was in the latter half of the 19th century, during the Civil War years, shortly before science became God in America, and the soul became a superstition.

4. The séance table.

One evening, in 1862, during a spirit session, the soul of a woman named Mary came through the medium. Mary told the group that God had given her special permission to come back from the dead to speak to them because she herself had been accidentally buried alive, not so very long ago, and she had woken up in her coffin, and died of fright.

Mary said that God never meant for anyone to die such a horrible death, so God sent her back to tell them that they were to go see President Lincoln, and have him pass a law forbidding anyone from being buried at all until their brain had been removed from their skull, and all the blood had been drained from their body. Mary and God had reasoned that it is better to wake up dead, than to wake up in your coffin six feet under. What do you think?

Through the channeler Mary gave them the day month and year of her birth, and the day month and year of her death. She gave them her Christian name, her maiden name, and her married name, and the town, county, and state in which she had lived and died. Also, Mary directed a spirit drawing of the church cemetery in which she had been buried complete with an "X" to mark the spot of her unquiet grave.

After the séance they had the usual follow-up analysis to discuss the unusual results of this extraordinary session, and to consider Mary's weighty request.

The 1850's and 1860's saw remarkable advances in scientific inquiry, and knowledge. With the discovery that the brain, not the heart, was the seat of the human personality, science began to take great leaps forward. At the same time, there was an equal and opposite rise in what was called spiritism; mediumship, channeling, and an insistent exploration of the unseen world. In the majority, Science and Spiritualism were odds with each other.

Just as Leonardo da Vinci risked death to dissect corpses for the sake of anatomical knowledge, participants in Spiritualism risked their immortal souls for the sake of knowledge from the unseen world. Opponents of the new spiritual experiments damned the pioneers of parapsychology as necromancers.

Mary's express need for God's permission to come back from the dead to speak to the living is a perfect example of the general attitude of her era. The King James Bible specifically forbids the living to speak to the dead. There are generational curses that go with necromancy. Read the generational curse lists in Deuteronomy. That's an education.

The Theosophists tried to balance scientific inquiry and spiritism by approaching their séances in an organized and methodical manner, and by taking copious notes at each event. They were not airy-fairy fuzzy-wuzzy space cadets; they were intelligent organized forward-thinking adults.

A physician did not always attend people who slipped into comas, or became unconscious. Whoever happened to be there at the time of death simply put their ear to the chest, or held a small mirror in front of the mouth and nostrils. If no heartbeat was audible, and no condensation clouded the surface of the mirror, the person was presumed dead. The stethoscope had not yet been invented.

If Papa was a little hard of hearing, or the mirror and the breath were the same temperature, it was easy to mistake the living for the dead, and bury dear Suzette alive.

This mistake was so prevalent throughout Europe and America that people became panicky en mass. The natural dread of death expanded exponentially, especially as cholera swept both continents, and so many recovering victims in the final stages of cold and coma were hastily assumed dead, and prematurely buried alive.

People feared waking in their coffin to face a second death.

They began to leave written instructions in their wills, and in other legally binding documents, as to the method of their treatment prior to interment. Some asked that their bodies be decapitated, or their heart be removed.

Others, like President Washington, left instructions requesting that his body not be placed in the mausoleum until three days had passed.

A hollow tube was invented as an accessory to coffins, so that if one awoke in their coffin they would be able to breathe.

Unhappily, this invention only fed the fear that people would awake, only to die of starvation.

Ancient cultures circumvented this terrifying circumstance by incorporating waiting periods into the death rituals. The Egyptians and Tibetans had their books of the dead whose instructions made premature burial impossible from the start.

Hawaiians and American Indians had a ten-day ritualized waiting period, a practice that later caused small pox and cholera to spread like wild fire and speed the decimation of their races.

Finally, an American invented a device, which he patented, to allow those who woke up in their coffins to communicate their living presence to the world outside.

This device consisted of a little metal ring that was placed on the index finger, or on the toe of the deceased. A metal wire attached to the ring. The wire ran out of a hole in the coffin, and up through a thin hollow tube to the surface.

When you woke up to discover yourself, not at home in your warm safe bed, but six feet below the cemetery in your own cold coffin, you simply wiggle your finger, and a little bell rings up in the ground keeper's building. Then they dig you out, and all is well.

In an ideal world.

The only flaw in the system was that someone had to be there 24-7 to hear the bells, so a man was put on duty overnight to listen for the bells, and that is the origin of the term "graveyard shift".

In reviewing the information obtained from the spirit of Mary, the group decided it was unlikely President Lincoln would see them; he had enough trouble on his hands already. Furthermore the Lincolns' son Willie had passed away recently, and he and Mrs. Lincoln were still in deep mourning.

It was all very well for Mary the Ghost to say go to the President of the United States, but it was altogether another thing for them to just up and do it, especially under the present circumstances.

Nevertheless, making sure a person was really dead before burial was a sound idea. The recommended method of removing the brain, and the blood was scientifically more advanced that any other idea so far, and they had solid verifiable information that could be proved, or disproved.

It was unthinkable just to let the matter stand.

If Mary was telling the truth, and her message really was from God, they could not afford to ignore her.

And given the choice between waking up alive in your coffin with nothing but a thin wire between you and a death God never intended anyone to suffer, or dying while you were unconscious from exsanguination, they unanimously preferred the former of the two options.

Everyone agreed a research trip to Mary's hometown was the most appropriate first step. Based on what they found there, they would then decide whether or not to approach President Lincoln's secretary to request an audience.

When they arrived in Mary's hometown, not only did they locate the churchyard where she had been buried, but also the map she had given them through the medium with automatic spirit writing was completely accurate regarding the location of her grave.

They found her tombstone and confirmed that the Christian name, the maiden name, and the married name Mary had provided in the séance were also correct. The day, month, and year of her birth, and the day, month, and year of her death exactly matched the information from the séance.

Not only that, but through the pastor they were able to locate her next of kin, and obtain permission to exhume the coffin. This done, they lifted the lid, and there was Mary.

My Aunt Hattie was buried in my mother Elizabeth's Prom dress in her hometown of Plainfield, Wisconsin. I stood over Aunt Hattie's grave with her diamond engagement ring on my finger when we buried Elizabeth's mother, Cora McLaughlin Macaraeg, my grandmother, in the family plot in Plainfield, Wisconsin.

My grandmother, Lala, grew up on a hops farm near Plainfield. There is a movie about a man from Plainfield, Wisconsin, who also grew up on a farm near Plainfield. His name was Edward Theodore Gein. Ed Gein. The serial killer. Lala was six years older than Ed, but her parents knew Ed's parents, and Lala said Edward was no good from the start.

Elizabeth stood next to me, and looked down into Aunt Hattie's grave, and thought about her Prom dress.

Elizabeth won't accept it, but I can read her mind from the other side of the planet, and there in the churchyard cemetery she was thinking about the last time she saw that dress, and what it must look like now.

"I'm having Eddie cremated." Ed told me. "If we bury him in The Sonoma Mountain Cemetery, Elizabeth will lie awake at night with visions of his body bloating as it rots to pieces."

Put me down for cremation.

Please.

Historically it was customary to bury a deceased lady in her best dress, and in the old days, that was usually her wedding gown. It didn't really matter if she had gotten skinny, or fat as the years went by; the practice of slitting suits and dresses up the back is still standard procedure in the quiet trade.

Mary was laid out in her wedding dress inside the newly opened coffin. Her Bible was there, just as it had been when they lowered her down into the grave, but it was not on her breast under her neatly crossed hands as it had been on the day of her funeral. It was shoved off to the side against the wall of the coffin.

Mary's body was curled up on its side in a fetal position, and her fists were crammed into her open mouth so violently that the jawbone had broken away from her skull on both sides of her face. Her eyes were wide open, and the cloth lining of the coffin has been frantically shredded. There was no doubt that she had literally died of fright.

This hard evidence put a new light on the idea of contacting the President.

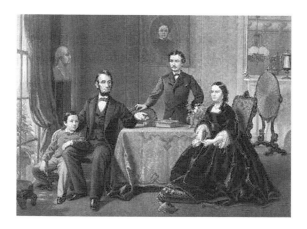

Mr. and Mrs. Lincoln received the group of Theosophists at the White House in record time. They had a tea with the President and the First Lady that lasted four hours. Unbeknownst to them, Mr. Lincoln was desperately interested in proof of life after death, and he had already conducted a number of secret séances in the White House.

Mrs. Lincoln was prostrate with grief over the death of her son Willie. She could not understand a god who let such a bad thing happen to someone as good and true as Willie had been.

Mary Lincoln's faith shattered with Willie's untimely death, and Mr. Lincoln was afraid she would go completely mad if her faith was not restored soon. He had prayed and prayed for a way to prove to his wife that the soul survives bodily death, so he could offer her the consolation of an eternal reunion with Willie.

President Lincoln himself believed very much in life after death, and it was already a great comfort to him. His recurring nightmare of walking into the White House parlor, seeing his own coffin, and hearing that "someone shot the President" is a matter of record.

President Lincoln is also the single most frequently reported ghost in the White House. It is reasonable to assume that the lives and souls of the young men in the armies of both the North and South weighed heavily on his heart.

Evidence of life after death could not have come to the White House at a more crucial moment.

A Federal law was quickly passed as a result of Mary's visit from beyond the grave, and the practice of removing the brain and the blood from the body became the national prerequisite for the burial of the dead in America.

We are the first people in the world to create a law that requires the removal of the brain prior to burial.

Except, of course, the Egyptians.

Americans accepted the draining of blood from the body, but they did not accept the removal of the brain.

Science had named the brain as the seat of reason and personality, and to most people personality meant soul, and removing the seat of the soul didn't go over well at all.

People were upset that their loved one was laid to rest without the good brains God gave them.

To address these ardent objections, Lincoln ordered that the brain must be placed in the abdomen, under the heart of the deceased.

This is the origin of the "Y" cut we see on TV; unless we are in the quiet trade, or in medicine, or homicide.

Allow me to apologize in advance to those of you who have recently attended the open casket funeral of a loved one, but when you see a dead body laid out for that final farewell, you are looking at a person with a head full of Pampers.

The people in Sonoma who buried out of the house that is now Deuce, and once chose their coffins here, have said their last good-byes and final farewells to their loved ones. Now they, too, have gone to Glory.

Their generation no longer blesses us, or curses us with its living memory.

The righteous indignation and moral outrage over the conversion of Sonoma's family funeral parlor to the Au Relais, or Magulio's, or Deuce, has gone to Glory with them.

The house that is now Deuce is now remembered and loved best for good parties, happy memories, and dinners, and lunches with friends and families. It is honored for the delicious food, for the judicious wine list, and for the great atmosphere created by caring owners and a superbly competent staff.

And this is how it should be.

For an elegant lunch, or an elegant dinner, or a special party, I recommend Deuce in Sonoma, and Maxim's restaurant, The Kenwood, North of Sonoma on Highway 12 right before you get to Kenwood. In both restaurants the food, the atmosphere, the wines, and the wait-staff are marvelous.

The gardens and the garden tables are especially wonderful, and well worth experiencing both by day and by night.

Deuce's garden is rather English and secretive, just like Harry, while there are wonderful views of the mountains and the vineyards from Max's garden, which is cool, and open, and fun.

Just like Max.

How It All Began

Mary Orlin is a smart attractive brunette with a great figure, and a smile that lights up her eyes before it turns up the corners of her lips. Mary is also the executive producer of the NBC show In Wine Country.

Mary Babbitt is the host of In Wine Country. She is fun, charming, and a real professional. She even makes learning about Napa Valley interesting.

In Wine Country is popular all over the United States. It has run for seven years, and will probably run for seven more, at least. Nowhere is it more popular, percentage wise, than it is in Sonoma.

As a town that was not on the Triple A map until 1978, it gives many of us in Sonoma a thrill to think that people want to know what it is like to live here. It reminds us of how lucky we are, and it helps us realize we exist to people other than ourselves.

This makes us sound like a bunch of fifth graders on My Space.

But, there we are.

You can imagine how amused and delighted Sonoma was when a big New York radio station had a national contest where first prize was two weeks in Sonoma, and second prize was two weeks in Paris!

Mary Orlin asked what attracted me to the paranormal.

"I wasn't attracted to it." I answered. "I was dragged into it by my parents."

There is a difference between the letter of the law, and the spirit of the law. My response was the literal answer to Mary Orlin's question, but what she was really asking was:

"How did it all begin?" And there is a different answer to that question.

It all began with a family outing.

On Sundays my mom and dad would pile us into the Yellow Bucket (my father's nickname our 1956 Ford convertible) and take us off the mountain in Mill Valley, where we lived in a rustic three-room cabin.

Sometimes we'd go to Old Mill Park, or Stinson Beach. And sometimes, always in the years after the house at 205 East Spain and first saw us, we'd go Sonoma, to the big town square everyone calls "The Plaza".

We'd feed the ducks and geese from the edge of the pond, and wait for the baby-ducks, bristly little balls of fluff and sunshine, to come out from under the old stone bridge.

The Sunday drive was the All-American tradition. With gas at 19 cents a gallon there wasn't anything that could give you a bigger bang for your buck. Especially when you didn't buy ice cream, or sandwiches, and you brought your own stale bread to nibble on, and feed to the ducklings.

Were we All-American? You bet. My mother, my two brothers, Eddie and Eric, and my pink-perfect-pearl of a baby sister, Bettina, were All-American.

Born and bred.

My father and I had been born in those mysterious lands Elizabeth called "Abroad".

"Abroad" was Germany in Ed's case; three days off the ship from Brazil where his parents had been conveniently sent to mind Henry Ford's rubber plantation, and raise Henry Ford's son incognito.

"Abroad" is my case was Santiago, Chile, where Elizabeth had been transferred by the United Nations after she met Ed at a bar called Rick's in Morocco.

Elizabeth worked at the American Embassy in Casablanca, Morocco.. Everybody went to Rick's.

Say what you will. I couldn't make this stuff up if I tried.

In America the majority rules, so we were a family of Americans. And we were being raised in the thick of the American Dream; a post-hypnotic suggestion planted firmly in my parents' heads after World War II.

Ed let Eddie and me call him Ed, and Elizabeth let me call her Elizabeth because Ed hated the word "Mom".
"It sounds awful." Ed told me with distain. "It makes you sound like the unwashed off-spring of illiterate American peasants."

111

Ed and Elizabeth thought modern, they talked modern, and they acted modern, but they weren't really modern at all. Their parents were industrial era Victorians, the mark of which was permanently imprinted in the wet cement of their respective childhoods.

It didn't matter how open-minded Ed and Elizabeth acted, or what witty avant-garde things they said. The unspoken truth transferred itself to our little subconscious minds like baseball park loudspeakers. They were what they were, and the funny thing was, nobody knew it, not even them.

Naturally, Sonoma, with its Victorian houses and its Victorian traditions, and its Victorian attitudes, was a perfect fit for them. It was familiar.

"Looks like family. Smells like family." as my brother, Eric Heine, is fond of saying. "Don't step in it."

When Ed and Elizabeth were children, they never lived in any one place long enough to call it home, let alone long enough for it to actually be home.

Their parents traveled. They followed the work wherever the work took them, and Ed and Elizabeth were helpless little hostages to their Victorian parents' fortunes, and also to their mistakes, and their misfortunes.

Ed and Elizabeth never had a real home, let alone a real hometown.

My parents were world-weary. Welt Getragen, in German, is what Ed called it. Elizabeth, as a French Literature major at Cornell, would have preferred to call it Monde Las. Welt Getragen means something like "globe trotter" only instead of trotting, you have trudged until you dropped. Monde Las carries a connotation of having dropped out socially due to boredom.

They wanted a home. They wanted a hometown. They said they wanted it for us. And that was true, but they also wanted all that for themselves.

Any All American Family, living out the post-hypnotic suggestions of the All American Dream, needs an All American house

By the time I figured out what was going on, it was already too late. Too late to say anything. And way too late to stop it. The long afternoons in the park got shorter, and shorter. The endless rides up and down the quiet, empty Sonoma streets got longer, and longer.

Sitting in the back seat with the hot Sonoma sun on my arms, and in my eyes, there were no more fluffy baby ducks, no more geese to feed stale bread, and no more fresh park lawns under the cool shade of The Plaza trees.

The hot stick of sweat on vinyl glued the undersides of my thighs to the red and white bench seats, and the Yellow Bucket plowed the empty streets of Sonoma. On, and on, and on they drove.

Elizabeth called Ed the "Great White Hunter".

How long did the Yellow Bucket sail the streets like the Flying Dutchman?

How long did we wait inside her metal belly like Pinocchio, and Gepetto?

How long was our crew of children held hostage by our very own personal Ahab?

You wont' believe me. I know you won't believe me, but I will tell you anyway, because it is the truth.

Seven years.

Yes. Seven years.

From the time the house first captured my parents attention to the day Bill Black tacked up a hand-painted "For Sale" sign on one of the tall white saber-scarred posts. Seven years.

For seven years we turned right at The Plaza, cruised down East Napa Street past Mr. Simmons' Pharmacy with the marble soda fountain; turned left past Mission Hardware's red bricks with the shared doorway that led into Brundage's; past the Sebastiani Theatre's forever-empty tile ticket booth. Then right onto East Spain Street, past the Mission, The Blue Wing Inn, and into the sun and shadow of the house at 205 East Spain Street.

With Ed at the helm, and Elizabeth by his side as "First Mate" the Yellow Bucket sailed, and hunted; a doomed Pequot, under the iron fist of Captain Ahab. We sat silently in the back, seen and not heard, like the loyal crew we were, and nibbled hard-tack duck bread, as much hostages to the "Great White Hunt" as Ed and Elizabeth had been to their parents' industrial migrations.

At the end, in the end, the Yellow Bucket always trimmed her sails to rendezvous with the house at 205. It was her first port of call, and her last port of call. Then they would park and leave me in the car in charge of The Children while they stood on the little spit of land that was the unpaved street corner of the Clydesdale horse farm. They'd stare at the house, and hold hands as the sun glowed a friendly warm gold over the tops of the hills to the West.

All they saw was the house. They couldn't see that the house was watching them. They couldn't feel that the house wanted to catch them, and use them, and eat them alive, bite-by-bite. They didn't know that the house wanted to catch, and use, and eat The Children alive, too. They couldn't hear the house as it purred its fake purr, and smiled its fake smile. They were stupid, stupid, stupid, and I hated them both.

The sun went down behind the mountains.

Then, and only then, they came back on board, and hove the Yellow Bucket away from the bad house, and set their bearings South toward the safe haven of our run down three room cabin; the only family home I ever knew with Ed and Elizabeth.

One evening, after I had gotten The Children into their pajamas and helped them brush their teeth and wash their faces and put them down for the night, Ed called me into my parents' bedroom. I was excited. Nobody but Ed and Elizabeth were ever allowed in their bedroom, their bathroom, or their living room and library.

Ed opened a book of famous houses from their library, and he showed me a sepia tinted line drawing rendered in brown India ink. I saw the drawing in Indian ink, but I saw another drawing, too, at the same time, like some bitter coffee vomited out onto the paper.

Either way, it was the house at 205.

"I bought it." Ed said pleasantly. "We're going to live in it."

A hot rock punched my heart. The air in my chest shrank and went as solid as cold cement. I could not breathe. Under my ribs lay a mound of graveyard dirt; brown teeth bit down on my stomach, clenched my windpipe shut, then leapt up to gnaw on the skull behind my face.

Ed looked up expecting, what? Praise? Pleasure? Thanks? I could not speak. I could not move. I could not think. All I could do was feel. The death storm burst, and my head exploded like red-hot lava from a live volcano.

I ran to my room, slammed the door behind me, and locked it. I felt horrible. Horrible for Ed. Horrible for Elizabeth. Horrible for Eddie and Eric, and for my sweet pink-pearl of a baby sister.

Worst of all, I felt horrible for me.

I saw the house, and the house saw me. I heard the house, and the house heard me. I felt the house, and the house felt me. I was good, and the house hated me for it. It hated me because I was good, and for one other reason.

I was the only one who saw the truth, and there was not one damn thing I could do about it.

The Art Of The Possible

"Oh," people would say to Ed, and to Elizabeth, and to me, "I love your house." And they would say, "I've always loved your house." And "You know, I just love your house." We heard those three phrases from so many otherwise intelligent people.

"Foolish virgins." as Eddie used to say.

Is it possible to love a building? Deeply, utterly, viscerally? To love a structure of stone, and mud, and rough-hewn timber? To love it through the seasons? Season, after season? Through wet cold rains, and dry hot summers? To love it through fresh-blossom springs, and leaf-dead autumns? Christmas, after Christmas, after Christmas? Easter, after Easter, after Easter? To love every rough pocked brick? Every splintered rail and banister? To love rough fence boards polished to satin by the droplets of half a hundred thousand rainy days?

The kiss of Southern sunlight and evening moonlight reflect through warped glass darkly. Softly. Slowly. Images of the past are held forever in weathered windows. This is the physics of glass.

Can the ground a building sits on be more beautiful and more precious, ounce for ounce, pound for pound, than any other piece of earth on this blue star?

Is it possible to love a building?

117

Is it possible for a building to love you?

I believe it is.

And if it is, then the converse must be true. It must be possible for a building to hate you. To abhor you, to detest you, to be revolted and disgusted by you, body, mind, and spirit. To hate you with every fiber of its being, for every breath you take, merely because you take it, and especially because it's yours.

Would not every beat of your heart pound out against such injustice, against such unfairness, against such perversion?

I believe it would.

Is it possible, then, for it to hate you first, and to want to see you dead? Or worse? To break your spirit, to defeat you, to debase you? To destroy the divine spark of your very life, but to keep you alive, and aware because it gets such pleasure from your torture, your degradation, and your pain?

Such a house would allow no hope, no faith, no final resting place. Not even in death.

Is it possible?

Good buddy, that's a big ten-four.

Gateways To The Sacred Valley

There are four main gateways to The Sacred Valley of The Seven Moons.

Consecrated Indian warriors guarded them seven months out of the year. For the remainder of the year, these gateways were guarded by low caste Miwok and Pomos, costal Indians; by origin, generational slaves.

By privilege; these slaves were servants to the sophisticated elite leaders of the Indian aristocracy, the Chiefs and Shamans, who came to Sonoma to consult with each other, commune with their ancestors, to ask the advice and counsel of the Star People who lived in the lights they called down from the sky.

Shamans were not only priests, but also highly trained specialists in ritual knowledge, and pharmacopoeia. The ways of herbal medicine were passed down through generations in the highly structured chant songs of oral tradition. Like most true story tellers, their function was to instruct and inform, not merely to entertain. The penalty for changing the chant songs and stories of the oral tradition was death.

Shamans began to study at the age of four. The profession was chosen for them by their elders, based on temperament, personality, manner, and talent, but not based on gender.

Control the pharmacopoeia; control the people. This is why China hates Tibet.

Westerners generally think of Chieftains and Shamans as being men. This common misconception was deliberately fostered by the Indians to protect their most powerful spiritual leaders, the women, from the Spanish invaders.

That all leaders must be male was taken for granted by the patriarchal cultures of Europe. The attitude was violently and fanatically enforced for a thousand years, and underscored with the brutal destruction of the pagan matriarchies by the strong arm of the Catholic Church; the Dominicans.

The Catholic Church is divided into three branches. The Jesuits, or the Society of Jesus, form the legislative branch of The Church.

The defining characteristic of these highly educated men is that they can rationalize anything, and like the Devil himself, they can twist Bible scripture in such a manner as to justify anything, and everything.

Jesuits almost always come from prominent, ambitious families with well-placed money and political power. They are ambitious men. They are the intelligencia of The Church. No women allowed. But anything else goes.

The second branch of The Catholic Church is the Dominican branch. They are the army of The Church.

They are like the American Navy Seals, deployed individually or en mass, in uniform, or under cover.

If the Dominicans had a motto for the ages, it would be: "Count on us, when it absolutely, positively, has to be burnt down overnight".

The Franciscans are the third, and last branch of The Catholic Church. Historically speaking, they were a fortuitous administrative afterthought.

Devoted to the Holy Spirit, good works, and obedience without question, the Franciscans are the heart and soul of the Catholic Church.

If the Franciscan order had a defining motto, it would be "Yes, Sir. Yes, Sir. Three bags full."

For The Catholic Church's secret explorations of South and North America in the mid to late 1400s, the Popes sent in the Jesuits. In the conquest of South America the Pope sent in the Jesuits. The Jesuits had the brains.

But when the Jesuits began to argue that the South American Indians were human beings with souls, not merely soulless animals as decreed by Pope Charles, cousin to King Phillip of Spain, they were promptly withdrawn, and replaced by the blindly obedient Franciscans.

The Franciscans were so grateful to be in the game at all, that they would never dare to jeopardize their position by thinking.

Regardless of the branches of service, the Catholic Church is a patriarchy.

There are some powerful women in both the Dominican and Franciscan branches of The Catholic Church. As nuns. Not as priests.

Amongst the generational matriarchies of the American Indians, there were more female Chiefs and Shamans than there were male Chiefs and Shamans.

The Indian attitude toward women puzzled the Spanish Catholic observers, and the closest they got to the truth was to report to the Pope and the King that the Indians "seemed highly protective of women".

In fact, the American Indians literally worshiped women.

When dealing with the Spanish, it was safer and wiser to have a male warrior stand forth, and act as Chief or Shaman, than to let the actual female Chief or Shaman be known to the infamous, treacherous, disease infested barbarian creatures from Spain.

King Phillip of Spain and his cousin Pope Charles were both dead broke when they first financed the expedition across the Atlantic Ocean. The Moors had just been overthrown and Spain was in chaos.

To understand Spanish foreign policy in the New World, both in the invasions of South America, and in the North American conquest, it helps to remember the basic tenets of their ethics and their belief system.

When the first ship from Spain arrived at the tip of the Pacific side of Brazil, they had on board a Jesuit priest. His first duty was to report back to the Pope Charles and King Phillip.

A rough summation loses many florid embellishments, and much bulk in the translation, but basically it went like this:

"Your Holiness; Your Highness: There are people here. Do they have souls?"

It took this letter two years by ship to reach Barcelona, where both Pope Charles and King Phillip were in residence. Their response was direct and simple:

"Do they have money?"

It took four years in transit to get an answer from their Jesuit priest in Brazil which was:

"Oh, yes, they have gold, and silver, and emeralds the size of goose-eggs,"

Then it took four more years to get the response from Barcelona, which was:

"No. They have no souls. Kill them all, and send the loot home."

This is the foundation upon which all matters of Spanish diplomacy were based, and why there are discrepancies in reports of the exact year when the Spanish conquest of South America began.

Spain says the conquest began when they landed, and England says it began when permission was granted to rape, pillage, and burn, but Brazil says it didn't start until the first native death on Brazilian soil.

It's no use asking the Portuguese; they refuse to discuss it.

So, there you are.

The South American Indians used llama wool to weave their holy tapestries, which were guarded by warriors, and tended by the virgins at the Temple of the Sun. These rolls of woven wool contained the origin myths, the battles, the great events and stories of their people dating back countless centuries.

The loss of information that ensued when these tapestries documenting their culture and knowledge of pharmacopoeia were seized by Spanish invaders has been compared to the loss of the Library at Alexandria.

The history of South America literally rotted away on the floors and walls of Spanish castles and Italian palazzios.

You should excuse the expression, but Jesus Christ!

In the European courts, which included the Austro-Hungarian Empire, France, England, and Prussia, the court of Spain fell solidly at the bottom of the cultural hierarchy.

Spain had not been a civilized country for very long, and as far as the royal houses of Western civilization were concerned, Spain had yet to become civilized. Spain was the omega dog in the royal manger.

When the Moors invaded Spain from North Africa, they found a people living in the Stone Age. Spain had no agriculture, no irrigation, no written language, no domestic animals, and no skills with metallurgy of any kind.

The Moors taught the Spaniards how to channel water onto dry land. The Moors taught the Spaniards how to plant corn and other staple crops.

The Moors elevated Spain above their hunter-gather status, gave them a written language, taught them how to domesticate animals, how to make pots and tiles, how to fire clay, and create glazes and mosaics. And how to build houses, and move indoors.

Their only mistake was teaching them how to work with metal, and make swords, and other tools of war.

At that point the Spanish rose up against their benefactors, and drove them out of Spain with an unprecedented level of ferocity that stunned the world then, and still stuns the world today. If you are into horror, read Spanish history.

My FBI clearance to work with high profile and politically sensitive individuals, combined with the high-security training I received from Ron Southern, the former driving instructor who trained Clint Eastwood, Paul Williams, and Gene Hackman, made me the best candidate to drive for the members of the royal family when they came to visit Sonoma from Kuwait.

The September Vintage Festival is a big deal in Sonoma. It goes back further than the Fourth of July. We play rock-and-roll music, we dance, we drink, and we get wild. The birth rate still jumps nine months after

Vintage Festival, and July is the statistically dominant baby-month, just as it was before the arrival of the Europeans.

The priests bless the grapes, and everybody who disappeared into the vineyards for the Crush comes back into Sonoma like prodigal sons, and daughters, for the three days of Vintage Festival to drink, to revel, and to fool around.

Because I was the best choice to take care of the royals from Kuwait, I found someone else to drive the 1988 Lincoln in the Vintage Festival Parade, and I arranged for a Wind Star Van to replace the limousine. In Kuwait, limousines have sad associations because they are only used for funerals.

Vans are for fun.

One of the anachronistic disciplines of my teenage years was the mandatory study of Emily Post. Elizabeth had once worked at the Pentagon, with the Diplomatic Corps at the American Embassy in Casablanca, and with the United Nations in Chile before I was born.

Elizabeth harbored what she believed to be a secret ambition, for me to grow up to become a Washington hostess.

"WWEPD" became the formula by which all my actions were weighed, measured, and found wanting. When confronted with an awkward situation, Elizabeth counseled me to ask myself, "What Would Emily Post Do?"

Ed wanted me to be a doctor, and he got to me first. He made his goal for me clear by bringing home a crummy red plastic doctor's kit, instead of the beautiful blue nurse's kit for which I had begged, bullied, and nagged all summer.

"I wanted to be a doctor myself," Ed told me sadly, "but I was weak. I was too much a part of what I was cutting. I hope you will be better, and stronger."

I wanted to be better and stronger. I didn't want to be weak.

I stole one of Elizabeth's needles and a spool of thick black carpet thread. Three afternoons a week I put in, and took out, neat rows of stitches on the calloused heels of my little brother Eddie's three-year-old feet. I was six.

To become a Washington hostess never entered my mind. The Emily Post drills made no sense. Why bother to study all that when you live in California? One of the Heine family sayings, right up there with "Let's you and him fight" was "Don't confuse me with the facts; my mind is made up."

So, I studied Emily Post. Drilling me in the proper forms of address for Kings, Queens, Arch Dukes and Arch Duchesses, Dukes and Duchesses, Marquis and Marquises, Princes, and Princesses, Bishops, Arch Bishops, and Popes kept Elizabeth's secret ambition alive.

The good news was, if I ever met the Pope in Safeway, I knew exactly how to behave.

If the Queen of England and I happened across each other out in the vineyards on an arrowhead hunt, I was excruciatingly well prepared.

The royal couple from Kuwait had four hours to spend in the wine country, and because all forms of alcohol are forbidden in their country, they wanted to see, and have their photographs taken with, as much alcohol as possible.

In preparation, my mind rattled off Elizabeth's Emily Post lessons like an ambitious Catholic betting the farm on 152 Hail Mary's.

Kings and Princes are addresses as "Your Highness." Kings and Princes who travel incognito are addressed as "Sir". Queens and Princesses are also addressed as "Your Highness". Incognito Queens and Princesses are addressed as "Madame" with "Miss" for unwed Princesses, while "Madame" is reserved for married Princesses. Never say "Mam". Never comment without being asked to do so. Always use the proper form of address every three sentences. Less than that is disrespectful, and presumptuous. More than that is perceived as fawning, and will be suspect.

By the way, and while we are on the subject of etiquette, never address a Judge as "Sir". They train Federal convicts to say "Sir", and if you use it, the judge will think you've already done hard time. Always say "Your Honor" unless you are a real cowboy, or a real cowgirl, and then you can say "Judge". But don't say "Judge" unless you have the twang to go with it.

And call Native Americans "Indians" because the US Federal government lawyers say the US has no treaties with "Native Americans", but only with "Indians". That's why it's Indian Bingo.

"I am especially interested in your American Indian situation." His Highness said. "Please tell me, how do things stand at this time?"

Australians are especially interested in the answer to this question, too, because they "brought civilization" to the Aboriginals. Like it, or not the only Aboriginals interested in civilization are the ones who are part white.

"The American Indian situation is unfortunate, at best, Sir." I answered. "American genocide attempts were not entirely successful, and assimilation is only possible for a small percentage of the Indian population. Fortunately, every Indian with a degree in law is now works on behalf of the Indian Nation, so there is hope for them, Sir."

"My people confronted a similar situation when we entered Spain. When we withdrew from Spain in 1515," His Highness says, "we were uncertain of their eventual future."

"I understand, Sir. Spain's ingratitude and disloyalty has always been incomprehensible to me." This was a politic, but honest, answer. However, His use of the word 'withdrew' was an interesting and revealing choice. Withdrew.

How naive we Americans are when it comes to comprehending the way other cultures think. We think everybody thinks like we do. They do not. We think someday even China will think like we do. China will never think like us. If anything, we will come to think more like China.

His Highness tipped me $100.00 American dollars, and gave me a $100.00 bill from Kuwait. On the front of the currency there was a beautiful etched engraving of his face.

"Oh!" I said, examining the image. "Is this you, Sir?"

"Yes." He said regally. "It is."

Elizabeth's voice whispered down the decades from the dusty attic of my forgotten Emily Post lessons. I thanked her silently, and spoke the exact words she taught me to speak if I ever found myself in this particular situation with a King and his portrait.

"It is a handsome likeness, Sir, but it does not do you justice."

How wonderful it is to be in the presence of superior, elegant, educated, and royal beings! How fortunate we, their inferiors, are, to be near them! They can be gracious beyond our wildest dreams! They are, so truly, cultured.

Their Highnesses had global educations in history and politics, and a completely serene awareness of their own dominant place in world history.

Was I uncomfortable in their royal presence? Did I truly feel myself to be inferior? Of course! But I also felt grateful for the opportunity to have these feelings. These feelings are prerequisite to growth.

When I was 19, I finally gave in to the parental thumbscrews and dated John David Rothschild. After 12 sequentially sloshed Thursday night dates with his laundry at his parents house, I gave up.

Elizabeth was furious, and retreated to her room in tears, but not before she turned me over to Ed. Ed took me into the living room and gave me the You-Are-Not-My-Daughter speech. Then Ed gave me the Never-

Darken-Our-Door-Again speech. And he had just lunged into the You-Are-No-Longer-A- Member-Of-This-Family speech, when the whole house shook, and the lights shorted out all over the house.

While Ed was groping around in the dark, I skipped out the back door, and I was gone, Baby, gone.

For three long years I stayed gone. No contact. No visits. No phone calls. Not even a postcard. Then I became engaged to James David Zellerbach, whose family owned, among other things, the local Hanzel Winery. It never occurred to me that he had any money. Industrialists' fortunes follow a pattern. Generation one makes it; generation two maintains it; generation three spends it; generation four starts over penniless. David was a fourth generation Zellerbach? So what?

Nevertheless, as soon as they heard about our engagement, I found myself magically reinstated into the good graces of my suddenly delightful and strangely adoring parents. I was even invited to enter the house to see my brother and sister, Eric and Bettina again, as long as I was with David.

The oily alacrity with which Ed and Elizabeth welcomed me back because I was with a man who wanted to marry me was nauseating. But I'd been out in the cold for so long. I figured, forgive and forget. Besides, I was madly in love with James David Zellerbach.

"Foolish Virgin." as Eddie would have said.

When David and I broke up, you would have thought all four horsemen of the Apocalypse had arrived. Elizabeth was furious, and retreated to her room in tears, but not before she turned me over to Ed. Ed took me into the living room, and there on the Harold Burrell Memorial Sofa from Sloan's, Ed gave me the You-Are-Not-My-Daughter speech.

Then Ed gave me the Never-Darken-Our-Door-Again speech. And he had just segued into the You-Are-No-Longer-A-Member-Of-This-Family speech, when the whole house shook, and the lights shorted out again.

Alone in the dark, Ed said things that could only have come from the house. He used really nasty words in a voice I'd heard before when normal conversations went to Hell in the dining room of the three-way murder.

Ed used the F-words, and B-words, and D-words, and even a long spitting string of C-words. The snot-green orb was all over him like a Neon sign.

Then a lady-angel in a burgundy dress appeared by my side, and whispered into my ear.

"It's alright, Dear." she said. "It's not your father speaking to you. It's speaking to someone else. It's not him at all anymore now. It's something else; something from the house. Hold on just a little longer, Dear, and then you can leave."

While we were still "en rapport" David and I liked to use his family's box at the San Francisco Opera House. We saw every performance of the entire run when the Bolshoi had their first American engagement. The place was surrounded by both American and Soviet armed guards, because both sides had a terrible fear of defection, but it was an honor to watch the Bolshoi perform, and to meet such accomplished and dedicated international artists.

Ballet is a fine art I love, and I have seen every ballet performance of every traditional ballet as many times as I could possibly manage to do so. For every ballet I have seen from a seat in the audience, I have seen five standing at the back of the house in my tennis shoes thanks to SRO (Standing Room Only) tickets, which only cost $5.00. It is virtually impossible to add to that an estimate of how many ballets I have seen while they were still in rehearsal.

So I know something about the art form, especially after 35 years with Beth Marie Deenihan at the Sonoma Ballet Conservatory.

When the Bolshoi and the Kirov do Sleeping Beauty, the opening scene, where all the royal families attend the christening of Princess Aurora, is breathtaking. It isn't only the costumes, and the music, and the lighting. It's the way they stand, and move together, before the dance. The Russian dancers project the epitome of royalty. Their inherent understanding of genuine blue-blooded aristocracy is palpable, even though there has been no royal aristocracy in their country, for almost a hundred years.

By comparison, when you watch American ballet companies do Sleeping Beauty, the contrast is painful. Our most accomplished American dancers stand around, hip-shot and slumped, like they are at some generic corporate cocktail party in which they have no vested interest.

Our American understanding of the Indians and the Chinese and the Arabs is like our American dancers' understanding of royalty.

We think we know what is happening, and we think we know what we are doing, and we think we have a corner on the reality market.

We ignore what we should learn from the history of these cultures. We assume we can influence them with economic sanctions and coercion. We believe we can get them to behave and think as we do in America.

No way, Jose.

Fat chance, quoth Ling-Ling the pot-sticker.

There is no God but Allah, and Mohammed is his Prophet.

So, who ended up invading South America? The lowest, most morally and financially bankrupt, least civilized barbarians of Europe. The Spanish, and the Catholic Church, under the direction of King Phillip, and his cousin Pope Charles.

Who provides the ransacked blood-smeared gold that pulls Western Europe up out of the plague-ridden muck-sucking Dark Ages? Who finances the Golden Age of Queen Elizabeth with pirate plunder? Whose ambition destroyed the Spanish warships of the Armada?

Who made the Age of Piracy possible by attracting English pirates to the treasures of South America on the open sea? Who invented the Inquisition? Who invented forgiveness of sins for the Catholic Church in exchange for cash in 1540? Who left Spain penniless after the New World was stripped naked and destroyed?

The first three guesses don't count

When the barbarians from Spain arrived in North America, in Sonoma, in the heart of an 80,000-year-old social, religious, and political empire, did the Indians tell them everything, and show them their jugular veins, or did they provide information cautiously, on a need-to-know, safe-to-tell basis, while officially playing the gracious host?

I choose "B".

So does modern China when it comes to dealing with the US.

Attendance at the "High Times" of the October full moon Bear Sacrifice was not open to all. On the contrary, like today's Communist Party, it was by invitation only. The gateways to The Sacred Valley were heavily guarded; armed warrior patrols walked the perimeters; dog-runners relayed information from the four major entrances to the center of The Valley, and back again.

This is why, when the 1823 Spanish delegation of priests from San Rafael arrived at the gateway to The Sacred Valley where Klein Vineyards is today, across from the Jacuzzi Winery, at the Yenni Ranch, there were 10,000 well prepared, informed male Chieftains and Shamans of the Indian intelligencia right there to obstruct them.

The arrival of the Priests was a part of Indian prophesies known only to the elect. Initiated members of the Indian priesthoodknew the Spanish were coming shortly after they arrived at the tip of Brazil in 1515.

Inca runners quickly brought the news of the Spanish arrival, actions, and the avaricious intentions to come North from Brazil to Sonoma, but it took the Spanish 300 years to get here.

Their arrival in 1823 was the fulfillment of a 300 year old prophesey which said that when the Spanish priests arrived in Sonoma, it would mark the end of their world.

The Indians stood around and watched. All ritual and ceremonial practices ended. Everybody wanted to see these people who brought with them the end of the world, to get a look at them before they entered The Sacred Valley. Time stood still, poised between the two incompatible cultures, and the priests wrote in their journals that they had never seen such a bunch of lazy, stupid Indians in their lives.

The padres were so clueless that they thought this gateway was actually the center of The Valley, and they established the first Sonoma Mission there. Later they figured it out. Why did they make such a glaring error? They were "not from here", and nobody told them.

When the remarkable and accomplished ballet director Jennifer Bloom first moved to Sonoma Valley, she started her ballet school outside of Sonoma proper, and called it the "Boyes Hot Springs School of Ballet". She figured that out very quickly, too, but why did she make such a glaring error in the first place?

She was "not from here", and nobody told her that up until 1978 Boyes Hot Springs was the only drop-off destination for the entire Federal prison system. When convicted felons were released, they got a one-way ticket to Boyes Hot Springs in sunny California.

For decades, Boyes Hot Springs had the highest number of ex-cons per square mile in the country, except for the populations inside the Federal prisons themselves. Not a lot of ballerinas in Boyes Hot Springs back then.

But 1978 was 40 years ago. Now we play host to Witness Protection people.

When that pesky development group moved into town and tried to "eminent domain" the Leveroni Farm property to build a hospital out on Fifth Street West, why were they surprised when they were run out of town on a rail?

They weren't from here, and nobody told them.

People who come to Sonoma nowadays can feel safe almost anywhere> There's been no sign of the East-Side Rapist for a long time. But if you tried to enter The Valley without an invitation in the pre-contact days, you would be aggressively turned away. If you persisted you were killed on the spot.

Unless you had an invitation, you needed a really good reason to be admitted, and it required a lot of back and forth communications by the dog-runners to get special permission to enter The Sacred Valley.

These five gateways were strictly protected for two known reasons. There may be more reasons, but I only know of two.

One: To keep the evil shamans out.

Dig it.

Two: To keep ignorant people out.

The protocol in The Valley was very strict. Invisible, but strict. If you broke a rule, you were immediately put to death.

People who were ignorant of the rules lost their lives just for touching the wrong rock.

There was only one punishment in The Valley: Death. No trial. Death. No ceremony. Death. No chance to build up spirit power by suffering torture with bravery and nobility. Just death. Swift and inexorable. Death.

Like driving a car in America, entering The Sacred Valley of the Seven Moons was a privilege, not a right, and ignorance of the law was no excuse.

There have been so many deaths at the gateways, and the speed with which the uninvited, or unconscious were dispatched to meet their maker, and the blood-rituals for protection and entrapment combine forces to make each of these five gateways treacherous.

These places are both physically dangerous, and metaphysically dangerous.

Out at the end of Napa Road, by the old Stornetta's Dairy, across the gulch from Nicholas Winery, is another of these sacred Indian Gateways. Fatality statistics have been incredible there, so bad in fact, that Sonoma qualified for funds from the State of California to widen, bank, light, regrade, and rebuild that road, which was done as soon as Sonoma got the money.

There were no age-old societal prejudices to obscure the obvious necessity, unlike Stage Gulch Road today, and the Embarcadero de Sonoma in the past.

The old Embarcadero de Sonoma was one of the main sacred gateways. It is "down there" at the bottom of Broadway. Thirty-three fatal car accidents occurred down there before Sonoma was forced to acknowledge the existence of a problem. This unnecessary delay was due largely to cultural momentum and Victorian pressure against acknowledging the "goings-on" at the port, and the shanty town that grew up around it.

The town also refused to talk about "that place" "down there", because they were responsible for the deliberate torching of the shantytown, and the deaths of all the men, women, and children, who died in the flames.

"Let me tell this story." said the genteel lady in the back of the limousine one night at the start of a Twilight Tour. We were at the Embarcadero de Sonoma site, since this is where the first Indians met the first Jesuits on their secret sweeps up North America to Alaska in the 1400's. "I want everyone benefit from what happened here. Since he was my grandson."

"Young Kennedy was your grandson?" I asked, shocked. "I am so sorry! If I had known that, I never would have brought you here."

"No." she says. "It's all right. I want people to know how dangerous it is to drink, and drive."

She went on to tell the story of how her 22-year-old grandson lost control of his small car, flew off the road, and crashed into the woodworking building. The car blew up, and the flames burned the woodworking shop to the ground before the firemen could arrive to try and save the building.

The young man in the passenger seat took a lot of criticism for saving himself, and not saving her grandson, too. But that was patently unfair, since they flew off the road and rammed straight into the cinderblock wall.

He barely had time to unbuckle his seat belt and jump to save himself, let alone anyone else. It wasn't as though they had time for a pleasant little chat.

It was life, or death.

He made his decision in a split-second, and just in the nick of time, too.

This old port was a gateway to The Sacred Valley. It is metaphysically slippery, and its history as a port only amplifies the negative energy. You can feel it. Be careful down there.

Watch out.

It is more than haunted.

Seriously.

Down there, stuff can come in after you.

Stage Gulch Road, where Hwy 116 starts, is a gateway, too.

Sonoma has had so many deaths on Stage Gulch Road that again, we now qualify for enough government money from the State to widen, bank, regrade and rebuild, and hopefully light the third of the sacred Indian Gateways.

Stage Gulch Road is a killer.

It's also the only road to Petaluma, the next biggest town near Sonoma, so we have commuters who live in Sonoma, but go there to work.

We have people who do not ever leave Sonoma Valley at all, simply because leaving would entail passing through one of the gateways on the way out, and back through again on the way back home.

Believe it or not, when it rains heavily during the winter, Sonoma can become completely isolated, and nobody can get into Sonoma, or out of it.

Stage Gulch has always had a nasty reputation for killing people. In addition to its bloody pre-contact history, it was used as an ambush point in the Wild West days. Not only for robbing wagons, and individuals on horseback, and on foot, but it was an especially critical ambush location for the Wells Fargo wagon when it brought in gold to make the payrolls for the Chinese.

The Chinese payroll eventually became an irresistible temptation every time it came through. Vigilantes and California Rangers had the arrest of would-be Wells Fargo stagecoach and wagon robbers down to a science.

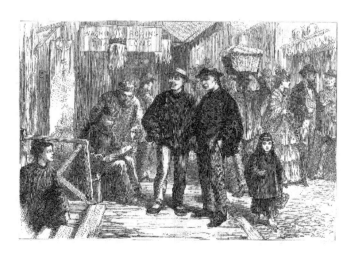

Part of the problem was greedy minds, and there were many men with larcenous hearts. Another part of the problem was the Chinese were not like the Americans. They didn't think like the Americans. They didn't mingle like the Americans. And they didn't spend their cash like the Americans.

This made some people really angry.

The Chinese saved their money; they never spent it on luxuries, and they never spread it around. They took jobs that the Americans could have done, and they did those jobs for significantly less money than the Americans would have demanded if they had been willing to take those jobs; which they weren't.

The Chinese worked for a dollar a day. Americans wouldn't work for less than $8.00 a day, and when Sonoma was short on laborers on account of the rush of most able-bodied men to the gold mines, the Chinese charged up to $17.00 a day, and people paid it. The Chinese took over whole sections of Sonoma with their meager little wooden shacks and dirt-floor shops.

Steal the Chinese payroll? Why not? They still had plenty of money. Stingy yellow monkeys. That was the general opinion toward the end of the 1800's.

The physical occupation of day-to-day Chinese around the Sonoma Plaza in the latter half of the 1800's was extensive. Wooden and canvas Chinese stores and businesses went from the Swiss Hotel all the way up to First Street West, then around the corner and all the way back up toward the quarries to where the houses stop. From the Plum Stone building at the entrance to El Paseo, to the corner of First Street East across from the Mission. Down East Spain Street, behind The Blue Wing Inn, across the Berryessa property where they ran the old Indian fish ponds, and all the way down to where Pete Viviani's house stands today. And from Turkey Street all the way along behind the railroad depot from First Street East to First Street West.

144

That was all Chinese. It was finally put to the torch and fireswept, but at one time, in this "one acre town with an eight acre Plaza", "them Chinee" were taking up about four acres right in the middle of Sonoma. Not to mention the Chinese tunnels and the underground city.

Stage Gulch is out by the dumps. It's narrow and cold, and overgrown by spooky old shade trees drenched with Spanish moss. The dark creek water deepens the gulch every time it rains, and there are three damned tight blind curves.

"Diapers. I've gotta buy diapers."

It was 9:30 on a dry dark moonless night. My focus was on the road, and on that quick series of tight blind curves. I've been afraid of Stage Gulch Road since the first time I laid eyes on it.

In Sonoma, every parent with half a brain, and a son, or daughter, or a loved one with a drivers' license, is afraid of Stage Gulch Road.

It is a fine line between fear and respect, and like Neigel says in the movie Spinal Tap, "It's a fine line between clever, and stupid."

The thought about buying diapers wasn't mine. I don't have children, and I don't baby-sit. This was the unusually strong thought-remnant of a Mom who drove through Stage Gulch ahead of me. She let her mind drift off the road, and slide into shopping-list mode.

Her entire focused had to be on the diapers to leave that strong an imprint.

Deadly, to let your attention slide like that.

And all too easy to do on Stage Gulch Road.

Stage Gulch Road invites unconsciousness. Stage Gulch Road demands unconsciousness. Stage Gulch Road is the perfect location for an ambush. And the perfect ambush victim is the unconscious ambush victim. Oblivious to the danger. Just enjoying the scenery along the beaten path.

"Primroses here. Primroses there. Little arbor with the Primrose on it." As my brother Eric is fond of saying. "Don't look at the cliff!"

Next thing you know, your baby doesn't just need diapers; your baby needs a new mommy, or daddy.

Stage Gulch Road has a spring-fed well just before you get to the dumps. This was where General Mariano Guadalupe Vallejo and his men used to stop to freshen up before going on to the Casa Grande Hacienda in Petaluma. It was such a good place to stop that a small farm sprang up there. A pig farm.

The well had a sign on it that said "Vallejo's Well" but someone knocked it down. It's a dangerous place to try to pull over, but if you can, slow down, and get a look at the remains of the pig farm.

It is for sale.

146

Everybody knows Sonoma real estate is desirable, but I laughed out loud when I saw the "For Sale" sign, because the real estate company retained to represent the pig farm is Sotheby's.

Stage Gulch Road is physically dangerous and metaphysically slippery. It is the last place in Sonoma you want to relax. Unless you are picnicking at the pig farm, or taking a break at Vallejo's well.

The narrow spot in the road on Highway 12 between Sunny Brook Farm and the entrance to Kenwood is one of the Sacred Gateways, but it was never a troublesome watch for the Indians on guard there. Less traffic.

There is such a strong predilection to fly through this Gateway that police officers who haven't made their quota set up speed traps there. This gateway to The Sacred Valley is, metaphysically speaking, a breeze.

The last and least known Indian gateway to The Valley of The Seven Moons is the Oakville Grade at Highway 12. It is a long narrow winding road from Sonoma, which leads up over the mountains, and all the way down through the forests into the heart of Napa Valley.

Oakville Road was a secret path for Indians who were already welcome in The Sacred Valley. According to legend, there were no regular warriors posted there.

Giant rattlesnakes guarded that mountain, the Indians figured it was already well guarded by the Rattlesnake Spirit.

When the Spaniards arrived, this path was widened, first for horses, then for wagons, and then it was turned into a stagecoach road. When the trains arrived in Sonoma, this particular stage route was abandoned. It's windy and steep, but the views overlooking the Sonoma and Napa Valleys are well worth the effort. It's a blast in a sports car with the top down, or on a motorcycle.

Robin Williams, the mind-boggling actor, director, and comedian, built a house on this road. It is for sale at the moment. He had to build a tall wall around his house, because there are so many rattlesnakes up there.

Too bad Mr. Williams didn't take my tour before he bought property. He would have known that Trinity Mountain's original Indian name is Rattlesnake Ridge.

Considering the size and strength of rattlesnakes in Indian times, at least Mr. Williams was in the wrong place at the right time.

The world of the unseen often speaks to us of doorways, and portals, corridors, entryways, and conduits. The world of the unseen shows us metaphors of light and darkness, elemental energies, and parallel dimensions.

We are called to understand the deeper meanings of what we see around us through symbols.

The tradition of the oracle is to tell two-thirds of their messages in words. One-third orally; one-third in written language; and one-third is always left unspoken. This one third is not missing, but it does not come from the oracle; it comes from the seeker.

The seeker looks within to receive the inner knowledge which is already there, but which is recalled to consciousness by the words of the oracle.

Be mindful of the symbolism of the gateways that surround the Sacred Valley. Be aware of their deeper meaning as you go in and out of Sonoma Valley, especially if you go in and out of Sonoma on a regular basis.

Familiarity breeds contempt, and contempt cancels respect.

Gateways of Sonoma are now as they were then; energetically charged mainstream conduits that connect Sonoma to the world outside.

They are places that slip out of our normal realm, and out of time and space, as we usually perceive it elsewhere. They let things in and they let things out, and they keep things in and they keep things out. Master spirits guard these portals, and monitor the energy levels around them. But sometimes forces and circumstances combine to make controlling them impossible.

If you are developing your psychic and spiritual sensitivity, they can provide an opportunity to hone your awareness, but choose your time and place with care.

Remember, Sonoma has five portals, and five gatekeepers, but there is only one key master.

The gateways escalate and revolve. They are dangerous, wild places, from dangerous, wild times.

Even today, their primitive energy is alive, predatory, and aggressive.

Shared Visions of Sonoma

Some people are so strong in their psychic ability that they give off psychic waves that enhance, inspire, and empower others near them to see what they see, and hear what they hear. These people are called "Amplifiers" and their psychic counter-parts are called "Transmitters" and "Receivers."

Prem and Jason came into Sonoma as a part of their California coastline route with a group that sells fine art reproductions in oil on canvas out of Los Angeles.

They set up over at Maxwell Village outside of Sonoma near the entrance to Boyes Hot Springs, and I saw them there the previous weekend. They had a big white truck, and all kinds of paintings out in front of Park Point Spa, not far from McDonald's. It proved to be a profitable location, so they decided to stay and work the Sonoma Marketplace in front of Albertson's supermarket in Sonoma the following weekend before going North.

What caught my eye from the far end of the Market Place parking lot was a large reproduction of the Van Gogh painting Starry Night. I swerved my 22-foot long limousine across eight lanes of empty parking stalls and squealed to a stop in front of them. With an air of supreme indifference, and an assumed calm I did not feel, I got out of Lola and proceeded to slowly perused their other paintings, and eavesdrop to see how they worked, how well they double-teamed, and to listen to their spiel. They dressed like college students, but they were as smooth as any carnies that ever worked a midway. I sat down at one of the patio tables amid vertical stacks of canvasses to watch them work.

The crowd ebbed and swelled, ebbed and swelled, but they were not making any sales. People looked, and they liked what they saw, but they kept their mouths, and their wallets, closed.

Eventually, Jason and Prem took a break. They came to sit at the patio table where I had strategically positioned myself.

They looked incredulously at each other, shaking their heads, and rolling their eyes.

"Tough crowd?" I ventured serenely.

"The toughest." Jason said, and Prem nods in agreement. "I don't get it. Mercedes Benzes, BMWs, expensive high-end boutiques all around the park. We should be making money."

"You can tell they've got taste by what they look at," says Prem, " but we haven't had one single sale all day."

"How'd you do last weekend?" I ask, conversationally.

"In Boyes Hot Springs?" asks Jason.

"In Maxwell Village." I specify. Only half a mile away from each other but to a person who is Town, they are worlds apart.

"We did great. That's why we decided to stay this weekend and give Sonoma a try. I don't know what we are doing wrong. The town feels so right, so good."

"It isn't you." I say. "Sonoma floats on credit."

"But we take credit cards," says Prem. "Master Card. Visa. American Express."

"But you saw cash last weekend, right?" I ask.

"Well, yes, almost everybody paid in cash last weekend." says Prem, and now Jason nods. They look like college students who study philosophy and physics, but with an air of Hans Christian Andersons' Little Match Girl.

"People over there don't have as much stuff, but they treat cash like money. People over here treat credit like cash, and they don't spend a lot because they are so far in debt." I explain.

"What do you mean by 'floating on credit'?" asks Prem.

"I mean it's all on paper. Not everybody, of course, but you'd be amazed how many. If they miss so much as one payment, it all goes down like a house of cards. The Benz, the house, the kids' tuition. Everything."

"No." says Jason, incredulous.

"Yes." says I.

"Looks like we made a mistake." says Jason, and a dismal cloud of brown smoke settles over the two of them.

"It's an honest mistake." I say. "All the data points to a good location, especially for fine art. I'm sorry. But it's not your fault. Sonoma looks one way on the surface, but that's not really how it is underneath."

Prem and Jason decided to finish out the day, anyway, and hit the road early the next morning.

"By the way," I ask, as though it's only an afterthought and Starry Night has not been the only thing on my mind from the first moment I saw the painting from the other side of the parking lot. "How much is the Starry Night?"

"Eight hundred and fifty dollars; but we can let you have it for $800.00." Jason says.

"I have $375.00 in cash in my wallet right now, and it is all the money I have in the world, so no Starry Night for me." That's one of the disadvantages to pulling up in the limousine; you sell luxury, success, and the illusion of wealth even when you don't have two nickels to throw at a duck. "What time do you usually pack up?"

"Sunset." says Prem. "What do you do for a living around here?"

"Me? I give two-hour limousine tours of 13 sites of Sonoma's ghosts and legends. Sonoma was the political and spiritual center of the Indian world for 80,000 years. It's the Indian sister city to Cuzco, Peru. This is where the Star People brought the Indians in the Sky Canoe. This is where they did the annual Bear Sacrifice to call the lights from the sky, and commune with their ancestors. Until about 200 years ago when the Spanish arrived."

154

They exchange meaningful glances, and then they ask what I charge, and I tell them, and they ask if I would be open to a trade; a tour tonight in exchange for my $375.00 cash, and Van Gough's Starry Night.

Allah will find, for those He loves, a way of eating in Sonoma. I had originally intended to spend my money on food. Silly me.

I picked them up in Lola at sunset, and even though they were not boyfriend and girlfriend you could tell there was affection and excitement between them, and they had a connection that I could not quite tag.

Prem and Jason were attractive without being attracted. There was love there, but it was not a sexual love.

That's the definition of friendship, isn't it? Love without sex?

We made the rounds with the Embarcadero de Sonoma as our start. The old port is a great place to get oriented, and see the Northern half of the Inca Road that connected Sonoma to Cuzco.

We talked about the Inca runners who brought the news that the Spanish were coming in 1516, and of the days of Spanish rule, and leather export, and of the whaling ships whose oil lit Western Europe, and all America's lanterns, too.

Then we drove into town to the Mission. I started with the list of things the State Parks won't let the docents say, moved on to the Indian origin myths, the sacred hallucinogenic ChiCha, the Western worldview versus the Indian way, and rest of the information the State of California has obliterated from the minds and hearts of the inheritors.

We walk down to the empty lot behind the Mission to the place where somebody finally put in a real concrete sidewalk, and Jason stops.

"I can't walk here." Jason says, and he looks down at his feet.

"What is it?" asks Prem.

"This is sacred ground." Jason says. "I can't walk here with my shoes on. I have to take off my shoes. We can't walk on sacred ground without taking off our shoes. It's a matter of respect."

So we all took off our shoes, and we did feel better.

Free. Grounded. Open.

Now, I knew Jason and Prem were smart; I had watched them work. And I knew that they were intelligent; I had spoken with them. But even before I mentioned the Bear Sacrifice that took place here, Jason speaks.

"Here is the great bear." Jason says, and points to the sky above the spot in front of where the sacred bear holding-pit was. "I see him, on his feet, clawing up at the sky. He is stretching into his skin, into his claws. He is a man. A man bear. A man in a bear's skin. Stretching up to the sky. Whoa! He's so tall! Look! He's seen me. He's coming over to talk. Stay here."

So then Jason steps out two paces, and I see this semi-transparent man step out of the gray shadows of dusk, and he walks up to Jason, stops in front of him, and tilts his head down to talk.

Prem looks attentively at the two of them, and I'm going with the flow, as if this sort of thing always happens when we go on a tour. I'm pretending that I am not knocked right off my lily-white butt.

157

Imagine a warm Sonoma evening right after sunset, where the brown gold of the dry low hills washes the evening dusk with sepia. Then, imagine a shaded line sketch of an Indian man, tall, strong, wide chested and beautifully proportioned, all done in three dimensions of brown India ink.

He was majestic, but quiet and calm; regal; inwardly the center and liege-lord of all around him. Tranquil, not with the tranquility of the weak or submissive, but with the tranquility born of absolute undisputed power over all things, and a total mastery of himself.

"First, he wants me to thank the women for coming.," says Jason. That blew me away; this ghost had naturally gracious manners that put Emily Post to shame. "He honors the women for coming. He appreciates that you come here, and bring with you what you bring." Then they talk some more, and I can't hear what he says, but I can see him talk.

Jason's face tilts up like a sunflower to the noon sky, and the big Indian has something in his hands that he plays with, or works, like he is braiding leather or straw, and while they talk he alternately looks at Jason, looks at the work, and looks at Jason.

"He says this is where the men meet to sacrifice one bear each year. This is where the ancestors come from the other worlds to speak to them, and teach. It is a place of learning. I was right to take off my shoes. He says this is the holiest of holy grounds."

So Prem and I stand there a few steps off, and I can't get over how handsome and strong and gently powerful this man is, and my mind asks 'Would you have sex with him?' and my answer is 'What? Are you nuts? In a heartbeat!' and my mind says 'That makes you a necrophiliac, as well as a nymphomaniac'. I thank my mind for sharing, and ask it to go work on my book, Sonoma Ghosts, because I'm in the middle of something really important here.

"We will move on now." says Jason, and Prem and I put our hands together in front of our faces and say 'Namaste' and bow to the Indian King, and Jason opens his arms, holds them up out to the side, and leads us away like we just had a holy audience with the Dahli Llama.

Which is exactly what it felt like.

Once back in the limousine we are silent, thoughtful, and grave, so I cruise up First Street past the bike path where the railroad tracks used to run, down Blue Wing Drive, and right down Second Street East to Vella's Cheese Factory where we get out of the car for a stretch-break.

"What did he say to you?" I finally ask Jason.

"He told me some personal things I will need to know for the future." says Jason, totally frank, and open.

"Ah." I say, knowingly. "Man-talk." We all smiled. "I always think of how Indian legend predicted that when the priests arrived at the heart of Sonoma, it would be the end of the Indian world. It must have been a terrible experience for him to watch his people go from over 800,000 to 8,000 in the course of only three years. That's like watching the population of San Francisco reduced to the size of Sonoma."

Both General Vallejo and Sem Yet Ho survived the epidemic because the Catholic Church inoculated them. That gives you an idea how important he was politically. No other Indians were vaccinated. But how awful to watch the spiritual and cultural center of your world die off from the population of San Francisco to the population of Sonoma in three short miserable years.

"It was his destiny." says Jason in a soft, but matter-of-fact voice. "He knew it would come someday, and he was unprepared for it to happen in his lifetime, but he felt it was a great responsibility, and a great honor to be the witness of the fulfillment. That was his destiny before the foundation of the world. That was what he was born to do."

I admit, I wished I'd heard what Jason heard from Sum Yet Ho. The man-to-man talk.

One of the things about being a woman is that you never really get to hear how men talk when they are not in the presence of a woman. Being there at all when they talk means they are in the presence of a woman; namely you, a woman. So it is rare to get a chance in real life to hear men talk when they are not in the presence of a woman.

Watching Jason speak with Sem Yet Ho, for this is surely who that was, and there is no room for even half a doubt, was like watching two older brothers talk from a distance with their heads bowed toward each other in earnest conversation.

They were equals on a special level, with a long common history that I will never share with anyone, a history of being men, of being a man among men, and consequently being able to talk man to man.

Sigh.

Oh, well.

We talked about Vella's Cheese Factory, and the secret government experiment, which was conducted there, but nothing out of the ordinary happened, so we cruise on down to the corner of East Spain.

I park the car on Second by Castagnaso's Clydesdales' farm, we get out, and we all sit on the sidewalk at the curb across the street from 205, my parent's house for almost 40 years.

"How did you learn all this?" Prem asks.

Prem was seated on my right. Jason was seated on my left.

I was in an inter-galactic wind tunnel.

"I was in the right place at the right time with the right stuff." I said glibly. "This house, here, across the street, used to be the cavalry headquarters for the officers of the Spanish invaders in the early 1800's.

"Then it became the Mexican officers' headquarters, and after that the American cavalry officers were stationed here. My father did his military service in the last mounted division of the United States Cavalry, and he couldn't resist the house.

"He and my mother got involved in saving Sonoma's old buildings. The history of Sonoma is actually the history of the New World.

"I grew up in that house. My father was an architect, and both my parents were founding members of the Sonoma League For Historic Preservation. My father, Ed, was the city councilman who had all the electrical and telephone wires put underground around The Plaza."

Ed established Sonoma's Historic District and the Architectural Design Review Committee. It stopped people from tearing down nice old historic buildings, and putting up dreadful ticky-tacky houses.

"When we moved here, Sonoma needed lights for The Plaza. My parents opened the house to the public to help raise the money. We called it The Fifty Cent Tour. It cost $5.00.

People thought that was funny, and in those days the only way you got to see the inside of somebody else's house was if you were invited in, socially. They paid the $5.00 gladly, and came in sheepishly.

People were really curious to see the inside of the house.

Now I know why.

When we had enough cash, my mother Elizabeth ordered the lights. She picked the ones that match those chosen for other cities by the same city architect in Washington DC, and Paris; Pierre Charles L'Enfant.

"I got to know the history of the town and the people from the older Victorians who lived here." I added.

The twilight had gone now, and a dim haze grew like fog around the house. Ed used to flip out when he came home and found the place lit up like a cruise ship.

"I'm hemorrhaging money!" Ed would yell at no one in particular, and at the house in general. "I'm nothing but a conveyer belt for money! I'm bleeding to death, and nobody gives a damn!" Full disclosure: if you want the pool at 100 degrees year-round, you are have to pay PG&E.

"My electric bill was $600.00 this month, Carla. It's your goddamn color TV."

There is an old Chinese proverb that says the key to happiness is a short memory. My experience comes from the other end. A long memory can be a serious obstacle to forgiveness. Especially self-forgiveness.

"Look." says Jason, and a light comes on in Eddie's old room. "There is a young boy there. He looks like an Indian. He has straight black hair. His hair is cut like a bowl. A long bowl cut. He has black eyes."

"It's a Prince Valliant haircut. My mother cut all of our hair to save money. That's my youngest brother, Eric."

I look into the light of the room, and it expands into part of the street, and obscures that side of the upstairs with a picture of Eddie and Eric playing, and Eric happy. Eric was about ten, before the house set us up, and dove in for the main course, and the family took center stage on a silver platter.

People who met us as a family, in Marin, or in the City, always commented on how well the two children from Ed's first marriage got along with the two children from his second marriage.

Eddie and I were a matched set. Eric was like two brands of chocolate, one dark and one light. Eddie and Eric fought like Cane and Able, and that was understandable.

Ed and Elizabeth favored Eddie, to say the least.

Eddie died before Eddie and Eric really had a chance to get past the sibling rivalry stage and become true friends.

As for Bettina, who was almost ten years younger than me, Bettina could be summed up in one word: Perfect.

Part of our family dynamic was nature, but a big part of it was nurture. Eddie and I were the oldest of the four children spaced three years apart. We got Ed and Elizabeth's best first efforts at parenting while Ed was still at his most European. Elizabeth was still East Coast.

Eric and Bettina got Ed and Elizabeth when they were being California parents, with a cut crystal and brass opium hookah in the living room.

Eric and Bettina's only formal education came courtesy of the State of California in public schools, and what they learned by informal osmosis from our parents, which is nothing to sneeze at.

Eddie and I had private tutors, and lessons with Ed as our teacher; essays, assignments and homework outside regular school, because Ed' family traditionally educated their children at home, in their castles, or they let the Church do it. Ed said he couldn't afford to hire a full time teacher, and he didn't trust the Catholic Church to do it right, so he decided to do the job himself. Oh, boy!

Jesuits at Barcelona and Cologne had educated Ed, in an era when the intelligencia of the Church believed that God made man's mind big enough to house all the knowledge in the world. One of my assignments was to copy the Encyclopedia Britannica word for word. This assignment lasted from first grade to sixth, and even though it was a daily hour-long exercise, I only got as far as "Baskets."

To add further distance to the gap, Eddie and I went through The Bell Lane School in Marin County. Eric Erickson, the psychiatrist, designed the new syllabus for the Federal government. The Feds wanted more geniuses to create new and interesting tools. They wanted to use us in the future.

Somebody gave a cocktail party for Dr. Erickson, to celebrate the opening of the new school year. Mostly what I remember about the party was skirts, belt buckles, and sharply creased slacks. Dr. Erickson looked about a million years old. Way too old to be a dad. He looked more like an Egyptian mummy.

I studied his twisted old smile through the bottom of his Martini glass. Here was a father who actually moved all the way to California, just so his son could attend The Bell Lane School.

I was going there because of what Ed called "blind luck. I stared at Dr. Erickson's belt buckle, and ran his words through my head twice to make sure I'd heard him right. What father would move anything anywhere just for a kid?

I was six.

Dr. Alexander Graham Bell was long dead, but the school was named after him because it was he who first proposed this new model of education that would teach children how to learn, and how to think for themselves, and it increased creativity, and natural IQ exponentially, for some. Dr. Erickson actually had to invent new tests to track us. Eddie was in the 450 ranges.

No wonder Eric and I always felt like dummies.

Across the street from 205, where Prem and Jason and I sat, one light went out, and the next light appeared, and illuminated the space at the far end of the living room downstairs; the old War Room.

"There are men. Rough Men." Jason said. "In blue uniforms. One will become a president. One will go mad. It is a room with maps. People come and go with letters from far away. Letters in leather pouches that unfold like envelopes." says Jason. "I see a piano. There's a beautiful lady in a red dress. She sings. They take turns playing the piano to accompany her. She is turning the pages as they play. They are all around her; pressing close."

I could physically see this scene in the light as Jason described it.

I looked at Prem sitting beside me on the sidewalk.

"Are you seeing this like he is seeing this? Like I'm seeing this? In the light?"

"Oh, yes." Prem said gently. "It's all written on the light."

The light in the living room went off, and another light came up in the entry room.

"This is where they hang their coats and hats. They put their guns here before they go to eat, or go into the War Room. They stand here to talk. It isn't important." says Jason.

The light in the entry room went out, and a light came on in my old bedroom. It spread out through the eaves like a slow summer wind. There she was, in the East window's sunlight, brushing her long hair in the afternoon as we watched her from across the street at a span of forty feet, and a distance of a hundred and fifty years.

"They are traitors. They are traders." says Jason. "They are trading her like she was a side of beef, or a hock of ham. That's all she is to them; what they can get for her; what she can buy for them; what they can trade her for. All this time she thought they loved her. All this time she loved them. All this time they were raising her like a Spring lamb for the marketplace. And they tell her it is for her own good, but it is all for them. She is only real to them as a tool to use, and sell away. That's not love. She can't live without love." Jason says, and adds: "Boy, is she upset!"

'Yeah.' I thought to myself, 'Boy, is she ever.'

Jason and Prem nod, my bedroom light goes off, and another light comes on in the far upstairs bedroom on the Second Street side, in the West Wing. Eddie's old rooms.

"There is a boy here who is really smart. I don't just mean really smart, but he's, like, super smart. He reads, and he works with chemicals, and he collects…slime molds? Can that be right? He collects slime molds. He's about twelve, but he's really old for his age."

"Yes." I say. "That's my brother Eddie. He had a piece of paper taped to a series of open glass petri dishes that said: 'Do Not Touch!!!' I took a pencil and touched one of his little molds.

It pulled back so suddenly that I screamed out loud. He comes into the room, looks at me, looks at the pencil, and says: 'That's what the sign is for'."

As Jason spoke, I could see the people as he saw them in the various lighted rooms. It was like a stage set when the lighting director brings up one light over here, then drops it down, and brings up another light over there, and they fade from one part of the set to another, and you see different scenes in different areas of the stage.

It was a cross between "Our Town" where the dead girl goes back to revisit her family on her twelfth birthday, and "Titanic" where the light on the old sunken ship illuminates the different scenes from Rose's life on her maiden voyage.

At one point, I couldn't tell if somebody was turning the lights on in the house, and then turning them off again, or if Jason was the illuminator. But by then it didn't matter. What mattered was that I saw what he saw, and he described what I knew to be parts of the houses' past; parts which included my family, and parts which included other people, and other families.

"Prem," I said, "are you sure you are seeing what I'm seeing? With the lights, and the people, straight through the walls, and everything."

"Jason's good, isn't he?" she nods affirmatively.

Room after room lit up. I saw it all. Jason described the fat professor and the landlord's daughter. He narrated the three-way murder in the officers' mess, which was our dining room. He described the man in the muttonchops who would become President of the United States, and the girl in my old bedroom who brushed her hair and wanted to kill herself until the angel appeared to save her.

That was partly me, but I didn't say so.

Before that experience with Jason and Prem, I would have sworn on a Bible there was not another person on this green earth who could tell the story of that house better than I myself can.

One of the things I love most about my radio show, Strange Wine, is that I get to share what I learn with 15,000 listeners, and it is a live thing; it grows with time, and revelation.

What I love most about the Ghosts and Legends of Sonoma Tours is that everybody has pieces of our town's history, and our races' history, tucked away in their minds, and even though I am the hostess, the tour guide, and the chauffeur, I am constantly learning more and more, making corrections to my knowledge bank, ironing out little wrinkles to smooth the way for the straight truth as I learn new tidbits here and there along the way.

It is a rare privilege to make money doing what you love to do.

The process is accelerated by meeting people like Prem and Jason, not that I've ever met anyone like Jason and Prem. But I like meeting people with extraordinary gifts; gifts of memory, psychic gifts, gifts of insight, and family stories.

Before the tours, it could take years to unearth one solitary piece of information.

It took two decades from the day I first learned the local Indian origin myth to the day I finally found out exactly where the Sky Canoe landed. It took another decade to find out which constellation the Star People came from, and why seven is their sacred number.

170

People who go on Twilight Tours are open-minded, and intelligent, and they appreciate history, and diverse cultures.

I thought my market would be a mostly tourist market, and some guests have come from as far away as Canada and even Brazil to take my tour, but mostly the people who go with me to visit the haunted sites are from Sonoma, or from Sonoma Valley.

The main clientele has turned out to be local families; people whose brothers know my sister, or who went to Sonoma High, or who already took the tour, but they got so into it that they had to do it again when their relatives came to visit, or send their kids on the tour when they come home for a visit from college.

Word of mouth is the way to go in Sonoma. And word of mouth here can make or break a business.

We have an industrial strength grapevine.

The down side of that is, we also have industrial strength root rot in our grapevine, so you have to keep checking your information against what you know and what you don't know, or you can get really mixed up.

"Little grape vines here. Little grape vines there. Little arbor with the grape vines on it. Look out for root-rot!" as my brother Eric is fond of saying.

After seven years, no two tours have ever been alike. But the tour with Prem and Jason was a divine eye-opener. It made me wish I had chosen the spiritual path each time, every time, from the first instant after I left the clear white light of the big bang boom.

It went on like that all evening, and I thought 'I never want to part company with these two', and I knew that I never would part company with them, really, and that although we had only met that same afternoon, we had never not known each other.

There is a part of Jason, and Prem, and me that sits after twilight, and watches the house illuminate from room to room with the people who lived, and loved, and hated there.

Part of us still sits there now, as part of us sat still there then. We are a hologram in time and space, suspended over, under, around, and through the years before, and the years after the instants we shared. We are each cells; parts of that larger organism people call the human experience.

Prem and Jason and I hung in the framework of the time-space continuum; three yellow diamond dewdrops in the web of night, halfway between now and then, halfway between the height of our brightest inspirations and the depths of our darkest nights in the space Rodman Edward Serling calls The Twilight Zone, and which Van Gogh calls The Starry Night.

North, South, East, and West

The history of Sonoma echoes the history of our country. Sonoma is the microcosm in the macrocosm. Sonoma has perfect demographics.

Madison Avenue knows Sonoma well. Advertising agency executives follow who we are, what we do, how much we make, where we spend it, and what we spend it on. If a product fails the test marketing in Sonoma, that product goes right back to the drawing board.

Kiss your national marketing plans good-bye.

The first European visitors to The Sacred Valley of Sonoma arrived by ship. They were scouting parties of black-robed Jesuits secretly commanded by King and Pope to sail North in search of the fabled Northwest Passage to connect the Pacific with the Atlantic. They came in the 1400's, the 1500's, and they knew where they were going because they had Chinese maps.

Thank you, Marco Polo.

When these Jesuits arrived in Sonoma, the sister city to its counterpart Cuzco in Peru, the Indians built a small house near their most sacred place, where the Sky Canoe landed. It was the original start of The Blue Wing Inn.

Less educated Europeans arrived in greater numbers, and for a while there was a peaceful, but cautious co-existence with the natives.

The conflict over Indians as material possessions followed, and Sonoma became the center of the Indian slave trade. Then the conflict developed over territorial possessions, and further along the way came genocide.

The division between the East and the West, then the North and the South of our nation is echoed in Sonoma's history, too. We box the compass.

Europeans with loyalties to Kings and Pope, church and country, pioneered the West side of Sonoma, just as they pioneered the Wild West. The West side of Sonoma was the most acceptable and powerful side of Sonoma, socially, politically, and economically. This was "Old Money".

Then came the fall of the elite educated upper class comprised of powerful intelligent individuals like the founding fathers, and the rise of the middle class, which thinks of itself as a democracy, but which is actually a republic enslaved by modern feudalism.

The fall of the monarchies, and inherited money, gave way to the arrival of the industrial revolution, and earned money in the United States in general, and in Sonoma specifically.

The American Northeast produced factory money and jobs, and the South remained an oppressed society of people who had fallen from grace. Simultaneously, Northeast Sonoma prospered and became occupied by working class families and professionals, while Sonoma's Southwest side was agrarian family farms, with its roots still in the dirt.

In latter half of the 1800's respectable people in Sonoma occupied the areas North of Napa Street, and the little bridges that divides North from South on the East side took a person "down there". When the War Between the States began refugees from the South came to Sonoma and lived down there, too.

Down there was where respectable men from town kept their mistresses and their illegitimate offspring neatly out of sight. Down there was beneath the notice of their wives and daughters, and other respectable ladies of Sonoma.

Respectable ladies in Sonoma ventured no further South than Napa Street, unless they had goods coming in at the Embarcadero de Sonoma at the bottom of Broadway. In that case, they were allowed as far South on Broadway as Four Corners, about a mile from the Plaza, provided armed men, like their husbands, uncles, or fathers accompanied them.

The "unwholesome" past of early Sonoma's Wild West days is reflected by a lack of sidewalks, streetlamps, or even roads, on account of the Sonoma City Charter's rule about not having to pay for sidewalks, or street lamps, or roads on property where there had been "dicing, drinking, or whoring".

That let out most of the town, and most especially Second Street East, which was lined with cottages and houses and shacks occupied by the mistresses and their illegitimate offspring. Second Street East was Prostitute Row.

The impending War between North and South made it necessary to get California into the Union, so there would be gold to finance the Glorious Army of the Republic. Getting California into the Union meant taking California's capital; Sonoma. Taking Sonoma meant occupying Sonoma with professional killers who were totally loyal to the President.

Enter: Stevenson's Regiment – Company "C" – The New York Volunteers.

Getting the gold out of California and back to Washington D.C. meant building a Transcontinental Railroad. That's where the Chinese came in.

After the Civil War was won, Lincoln's trains brought civilized Victorian women with Victorian values. They arrived in Sonoma with their luggage, their baggage, and their self-righteous respectability unruffled by the rigors of having to get here the hard way, by wagon, on horseback, or by sea.

These women forged the Women's League for Decency, and pressured the menfolk into driving the prostitutes to the other side of the Sonoma River, which became El Verano, and driving out the Chinese, who ended up on the San Francisco docks at Portsmouth Street and started today's Chinatown.

The Sonoma prostitutes formed El Verano on the other side of the Sonoma River. Please note: the town of El Verano had no sidewalks or street lamps, or streets. The Sonoma Chinese, "Crocker's Pets" formed the original bulk of San Francisco's Chinatown population. In buildings where Chinese lived, they put cherry trees in their windows to signal other Chinese of their presence. This tradition continues today all over San Francisco.

Sonoma sailed through the Depression, due to the innovative thinking of Samuele Sebastiani, who converted his winery to a canning factory and provided jobs for growers, pickers, canners, and packers, not only for local people, but also for hobos at the end of the line, and sometimes at the end of their rope.

Although he received one of two licenses to make wine in California for the churches, it was Sonoma's backyard orchards, and a level of

176

cooperation born of desperation, that pulled Sonoma through the 1930's.

Isolated first by a reassignment our State capital over to Sacramento, where the gold was, next by the 1906 Earthquake which took Sonoma from three feet above sea level to 84 feet above sea level and cost us our port, and lastly by the nocturnal abscondance of the county records to Santa Rosa which cost us our position as county seat, the evolution of Sonoma as a town remained pretty much in the Victorian era from the 1870's until the late 1970's. The people with the money ruled, and those people were the Victorians. And the Victorians were white Anglo-Saxon Protestants.

As Sonoma became a commutable distance from available work, more and more newcomers looking for a hometown to call their own arrived in Sonoma in the 1980's.

More and more of them wanted to know why they didn't have sidewalks, or if they did, why their sidewalks didn't match the rest of the sidewalks, or how come their neighbor had an nice long bed for flowers, and they had dirt, or brick, or grass, or whatever.

To complicate matters, the City Council, formerly known as the City Fathers, passed a ruling that turned all the sidewalk areas within so many feet of the pavement into property that is now owned by the City of Sonoma, and that includes the trees.

Newcomers wanted to know why they had to pay for the flowers, and gravel, or the trees and grass, and the water to water said trees and grass, if it all legally belongs to the City of Sonoma.

Finally, the City Council passed another rule that requires people who buy a house to pay to put in the missing sidewalks. This sidestepped the whole sordid issue of the property's past at the new owners' expense.

Who worries about why, when you are faced with coming up with thousands of dollars?

Putting in a new sidewalk, which legally belongs to the City after you finish it, is an expensive project. It can add anywhere from $8,000.00 to $15,000.00 to the purchase price of a house in Sonoma.

The general attitude of people who are from here is, if they can afford to buy a house here, then they can afford to pay to put in a sidewalk, and, besides, it's not my problem.

Not very flattering, but very true.

Newcomers have the right to petition for a waiver, but not all newcomers read the fine print, and if people like you, they will take you aside, or call you up out of the blue, and tell you in person.

But if they don't like you, you are on your own, Baby.

And who approves, or disapproves the waiver? The City Council members who are mostly long-term residents, and those who do not have a sidewalk prudently decline to vote.

So we don't tell newcomers that the reason they have no sidewalk is because of a hundred year old prejudice against drinking and prostitution, or that the property has a history of "goings on."

If they knew it's really the town's fault that they have no sidewalk, and that they have to foot the bill for a hundred year old Sonoma prejudice, they might want Sonoma to pay for it.

Heaven forbid!

As you drive slowly down Second Street, look closely from left to right, and you will see just how much of that street was involved in illicit gambling, drinking, and housing the mistresses and prostitutes who were beneath the notice of the wives.

Consider that men who were "down there" had twice the testosterone of men today, and twice the oxygen intake to their brains. That is a scientific fact. In fairness to the men, it is important to remember that the only reliable method of birth control in those days was strict abstinence, and many respectable wives found the physical act of love repugnant to their "finer feminine sensibilities."

There were economic factors to be considered as well. A child born by a man's wife was a financial and moral responsibility, which many men could not afford. A child born of a prostitute was the prostitute's responsibility. Besides she was a whore, and the child was a bastard. Anyway, besides, it wasn't their problem.

The proper term for such unfortunate innocents, if one must speak of them at all, was "brats". It is a word we use today without thinking for even half a nanosecond of these poor illiterate, and illegitimate children.

"Geek" is used all the time, too, but not long ago it was the name for the man in the side-show freak tents who bit off the heads of live chickens; usually an otherwise unemployable alcoholic who was paid in whisky. Today it is a violation of Federal, State, and County laws throughout America to employ a geek.

English usage changes overnight, but have you ever tried to explain to a child why the term "sucks" is inappropriate?

There are relevant connections here about how harshly we divide ourselves from unity by our use of labels, and by negative judgments against our places of origin, and by all kinds of circumstances beyond anyone's control. Much that divides people are outdated dead beliefs.

In early Sonoma, East and West were divided, too. The rich people lived on the West side of town. They had inherited money, and Spanish land grants. The poor people who had to work for a living like doctors, lawyers, and ships' captains, lived on the East side of town. Then came the Gold Rush, and the new instant economy of found money turned the rules upside down.

Sacramento was soon named the new American capital of California; the closer the central government was to the gold the better for the Union Army.

Sonoma might have withered away after the gold rush. Spanish rule had fallen to Mexico, and Mexican rule had fallen to the Bear Flag Republic, and the Republic fell to the American Invasion, but even though Sonoma was no longer the capital of California, it still had the best of the bad.

By 1948 Sonoma had 128 houses of prostitution, and only three churches. Sonoma had the best whiskey, the best wine, the best food, the prettiest prostitutes, and the best of Paris fashion, and to top it off, everybody paid in gold.

Today the invisible boundaries are melting, and we tend to see ourselves as all one town, all one people, and all one interdependent world. This bodes well for the macrocosm.

Unfortunately, the economic fate of the world does not lie in the hands of Sonoma. Like the carefully orchestrated charade played out at Sutter's Fort to announce the presence, not the discovery, but the presence of gold in California, and like the carefully orchestrated charade of the 21 day Bear Flag Republic, the future of the global economy is wielded by a few select people with a firm generational hold on the hidden purse strings of the world.

They don't care who rides the throne for two or three decades, or who sits in the big chair in the Oval Office for four short years. All that really matters to them is power. Power, and the daily decision made every morning by the five men in England who set the price of gold.

Strange Wine

A thoughtful soul who lives in wine country has many opportunities to ponder the metaphor of wine. It is a powerful image, full of zounds and furry, zignifying zome zing.

The single most important thing I learned from my obligatory wine tasting certification for concierges, courtesy of John and Doreen at the Sonoma Hotel, was that when you look at wine under an electron microscope, you will be able to see the actual molecular structure of the apricot, the apple molecules, the citrus molecules, and these are what the unschooled palate gropes to identify.

"I taste cherry." the wine snobs used to say, twirling the wine around inside the bowl of their glasses and holding it up to the light; squinting their eyes, and peering into it vaguely, as a Gypsy might peer into a magic crystal ball. Then their head would sway in my direction, their eyes refocused on me and they'd ask: "Do you taste cherry?"

"I drink tequila." I'd say. "What's your point?"

Thanks to John and Doreen's commitment to educating their Sonoma Hotel staff, I learned that these people were not simply pretentious asses. They really did taste cherry, apricot, and even wet dog. Go online, print yourself a wine wheel, open a bottle of wine, and give it a spin.

There is something strange and magical about the way plain grape juice transforms to contain real elements of our loveliest most delicious fruits and berries from all over the planet.

Wine has a mystical element, a spiritual element that has yet to be defined. It may defy definition, in truth, because words are meager symbols for complex multi-dimensional realities.

Saturday night from 11:00 PM to midnight for the last five and a half years I have been in the chair, on the air, live on KSVY 91.3 FM. There were times I was ill, and ran a pre-recorded show, but there have also been times when, I swear to God, the Sonoma Vortex conspires against me. The radio station is a mere three blocks from where I live, and you wouldn't believe how hard it can be to travel those three blocks when the Vortex is against you. It has defeated my best efforts on more than one occasion.

"Strange Wine" is the name of my radio show. "Strange Wine – History and the Paranormal in The Valley of the Moon". The title "Strange Wine" is a tribute to Harlan Ellison who wrote an anthology of short science-fantasy stories by that name. Ellison's book is out of print, but find it, and read it. Like Heinlein and Sturgeon, Ellison's works are the dinosaur bones of modern science fiction.

KSVY is the first public radio station Sonoma has ever had. Sonoma is in a funny pocket, and in the fifties and sixties we didn't get more than a few radio stations, and even fewer TV channels. In 1988, when I was a chauffeur's apprentice under the tutelage of Ron Southern, who occasionally drove for Tommy Smothers, our Lincoln limousine was exactly like my limousine, Lola; same color, same make, same model. She had a clunky mobile phone, state of the art for the time, and the only way you could order a pizza from Mary's on that phone was to drive the limousine to the top of Old Winery Road, and call from the top of the Buena Vista parking lot.

You can imagine how thrilled we all were to get cable, and cell phones, and now we even have a radio station!

I was the third person KSVY accepted to produce a show. I got the late night spot I wanted, opposite my hero and abstract mentor George Nory, on Coast To Coast AM. George kept me sane through the long black nights after my second divorce.

The black nights actually lasted longer than the marriage.

George kept me company until the witching hour passed. I was hyper-vigilant, on red-alert from 11:00 at night to 3:30 in the morning. I kept my hands busy with sewing, knitting, and embroidery while George kept my mind busy with Shadow People, UFO stories, and information from the bleeding edge of science's outer limits.

I would have been clinically paranoid if my Ex, the new Jesus Christ, and his Lady Love, the new Mary Magdalene, had not recently come into a delayed telepathic puberty, and begun to practice their unhoned skills on me.

It would have been moot, if I hadn't spent the Fall of 1955 in that gray steel canyon they call The Valley of the Shadow of Death, where I developed walls where other people have no walls, and lost walls most other people have for life. And, vigilance would have been unnecessary, if I'd never known the Smiling Man.

I have no sense of safety in the dark.

Most people are afraid of the dark. People of every age. We tell ourselves we aren't, but we are. We get used to the dark, and after decades where nothing bad happens in the dark, we gain confidence from the repetition of uneventful non-experience. We still fear the dark.

That fear is there for a reason.

The Smiling Man taught me an unnatural lesson. My consequent ability to estimate just how bad things can be when they come at you out of

183

the dark, and the levels of violence and evil that can come at you out of the dark, has been enhanced, and expanded. The Smiling Man left me with powers and abilities beyond those acquired by normal life experience.

The KSVY radio show appeals to me because you are in a safely locked box in the dark, talking to like-minded people, intelligent people who, by the very nature of radio, listen to you, and hear you. You have a chance to provide information that will help them understand secrets that society keeps in the dark, and why they may feel as they do, especially in Sonoma.

"Do you think you'll be able to talk for a whole hour?" the new station's manager asked me.

"Oh," I answered matching his sincerity while keeping a straight face. "I think I can manage it."

"I'm not sure you realize how long a whole hour on the air really is." he said.

"My adult-ed lectures at the high school run three hours. I'll be ok."

Creating Strange Wine was the first new thing I did for myself, by myself, after the divorce. It took courage. It took nerve. It took part of the edge off being dumped and left for dead three months after our beautiful candle-lit wedding at the Mission.

Nineteen years, one month, and thirteen days had passed since I married Mike Deenihan at the sky blue chapel of the MGM Grand Hotel in Reno, Nevada. Julie Sedgwick was my maid of honor; Jessica Sedgwick, my flower girl; Richard Sedgwick, ring bearer. Buss Sedgwick was Michael's best man. That was the guest list.

I chose "Amazing Grace" for the taped music, but I just found out two weeks ago that "Amazing Grace" is a funeral march. Oops!

As Mr. And Mrs. Michael Deenihan, we had our picture taken with the original MGM lion who was practically a bag of bones by then, although he was still alive. His hair was matted flat, and he smelled like bad art. I felt sorry for him; living in a hotel. He was rescued when the hotel burnt down, shortly after our wedding.

By contrast, my second wedding was here in Sonoma at the Mission with over 250 guests. My girlhood dream had been to marry Michael Deenihan at the Mission, but hey, you go with the flow.

We had 36 angelic flower girls, all much-loved students from Saint Francis, and Beth Marie Deenihan and Carolyn Smith coordinated them, my two best friends. The groom I'd known, loved, and trusted for 13 years; Michael (Yes, another Michael) Andreas Heinzsch, musician, composer, and church organist for over a decade at Saint Francis of Assisi in Concord.

The Mass was conducted by Father David in full Greek Orthodox regalia, was spoken in Latin, German, and English for our guests from three continents.

Diego Garcia sang exquisitely, for God, and the rest of us got to listen in. Nigel Armstrong made his violin sing straight from the center of his heart.

"What are you doing with my grandson?" Michael's Opa Adolph asked me. "Our ancestors were still digging for potatoes when your ancestors were writing and speaking Latin."

It was a generational promise I made before the foundation of time, to "take care of him", and "see him safely married". My ancestor promised to marry one of his ancestors. She got pregnant, got sick, and he left her, forsaken, to die alone. She haunted the family for generations, preceding each death, and she carried white gloves if it was a female who was to die, and black gloves if it was to be a male member of the family. But how do you explain that to someone whose ancestors were potato people?

Besides, what could be safer than marrying me?

The chalice was Florentine, wrought of gold and silver. It was a gift to Father David from the Bishop of Rome. Michael Heinzsch and I were the first to use it. The experience was transcendent, but the wine was strange.

As we crossed the threshold, on our way out of the chapel, Michael let go of my hand.

"There's a bad fairy in this mix." My Guardian Angel said.

"And I'm going to find out who it is." I responded.

I walked out the chapel door, and it closed slowly, and heavily behind me. There was nobody out in front of the chapel on the dark street, or sidewalk, except Mary Bailey. George Bailey's ex-wife. She was standing in the shadows.

Mary Bailey was not on the guest list.

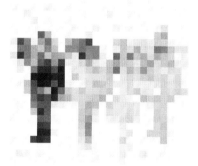

Michael Heinzsch and I were very happily married for three months, but on the first day of the fourth month, two weeks after Ed died of cancer at the Veterans Administration Hospital in San Francisco, Michael played his organ for a hippie wedding out at the ever-so-hip Ecology Farm.

Ken Brown, our once and future mayor, officiated, and even baked a salmon. After the ceremony Someone Who Shall Remain Nameless brought Michael a beer from the bar, and he drank it. Twenty minutes later the leaves on the trees began to wave to him.

Michael heard the grass grow all around him. A bright white light came out of the sky, and in it was the voice of God. And God said:

"Go to Mary Bailey. You are my new Jesus Christ, and she is your Mary Magdalene."

Telegraph the Vatican.

It was March 18th, 2002, at four o'clock in the afternoon when Michael Heinzsch got hit on the head with the white light. I was at our apartment on West First Street, and I heard the sonic boom all the way across town from the Ecology Center on Seventh Street East.

I didn't know what it meant, but a black tornado started to build in my solar plexus, and I had to act, or implode. I took out a jumbo roll of giant Hefty garbage bags, and tossed out every single article of clothing that I had ever worn for him. By the time Michael got home there were eight huge stuffed black bags lining the wall between our apartment, and the carport dumpster.

"Are you moving out?" Michael asked apprehensively when he saw them.

"Do you think I should?" I asked him flatly.

He told me what happened with the beer, the grass, the white light, and The Voice.

"Did you eat any brownies?" I asked. "Did you eat any mushrooms? Did you drink from an open container?"

"Why are you asking me these questions?" he asked.

"Because I was a teenager in the Sixties, and these are the questions you ask in a situation like this. It sounds like you got spiked. A big shipment of heavy-duty black market hallucinogenic methamphetamine came into Sonoma from Thailand last week. The receiver was on your guest-list."

"How would you know that?" he asked.

"It's a small town." I said.

"It wasn't that." Michael said defensively. Like he'd know.

Foolish virgin.

"It's funny God said all that stuff to you, Michael." I said.

"Why is it funny?" he asked.

"Because He hasn't said a word to me."

But He had. I simply hadn't listened.

We were furious with each other, and with ourselves. Of course, I handled it extremely well under the circumstances.

As hard evidence of my epic self-restraint, I offer up the fact that both Michael Heinzsch and Mary Bailey still live and breathe today.

Happily, these things can change overnight.

Bitter? A tad. But he was obviously out of his mind. How could anyone in his or her right mind leave me for a woman who loved "My Big Fat Greek Wedding" so much, she decided to live it as her life-script tutorial?

There was a cold comfort in the fact that Michael Heinzsch was worse off than I. I'd lived through Eddie's death. I had survived Ed. And I had been through the divorce from my First Love, Michael Deenihan.

In the old days, in the days of the tall ships, the whaling vessels, and the Spanish galleons, it was a fact of life at sea that a sailor who had already survived one shipwreck had an 100% better likelihood of surviving a second shipwreck. A sailor shipwrecked for the first time only had a fifty-fifty chance of survival.

Remember that monastery in India where the monks hang themselves from meat hooks to prove their faith? To manifest mind over matter?

Thousands of them died impaling themselves on the meat hooks before the first monk actually did it, and survived unscathed. After him, not one person ever died doing the meat-hook trick again.

"You march yourself right into your bedroom, and get down on both your knees, and Thank God Michael left you." said Philip Tarnofsky, the astounding Russian-American photographer who is my best male friend. Philip is brilliant. Phillip is talented.

Philip is smart.

I did exactly what he said, and I cried.

Mary Bailey was George Bailey's ex-wife and mother of his three children. They even had a son named George Bailey, and daughters just like George and Mary Bailey in my favorite movie "It's a Wonderful Life".

This was a sign, if ever there was one, but it ruined the movie for me, and I haven't seen it since.

In Buddahism, all eight of Buddah's paths to enlightenment start out with "It is Difficult." It's genteler than "Thou Shalt Not" and it leaves more wiggle room, too. Letting my favorite movie be ruined for me just because of the Bailey situation comes under Buddah's path where "It is difficult to overcome your personal past." Give me time.

190

"Look, Michael," I said, "if this really is from God, then it's the best thing for both of us."

Michael and Mary Bailey were married in Glen Ellen on February 14th, 2003, three days shy of what would have been our first wedding anniversary. They were married in the office of Jim Shere, by Jim Shere. Jim Shere had been our marriage counselor.

It turned out that Jim Shere was Mary Bailey's marriage counselor, too.

I heard about their official Las Vegas wedding that Valentine's Day, from Jeff at the Shell station on the corner of Patten and Broadway. I went there to fill up Lola after a romantic Twilight Tour for two. Halfway through that tour my guests rolled up the privacy window and we just cruised. Easy money. Bad news..

When I got home I e-mailed Jim Shere.

"You have failed Michael, and you have failed Me." my e-mail said. "You have failed your patient, Mary Bailey, and you have failed that unborn child!"

"You don't blame the dentist when the patient goes out and gets more cavities, Carla." He e-mailed back.

"Jim?" I e-mailed in response, "Can you spell Prophylactic?"

191

The moral of the story? Man proposes, and God disposes.

I knew the job was dangerous when I took it.

When you invite the Holy Spirit into your life at the High Mass, and you turn your future over, into the hands of Jesus Christ, it's like inviting a team of contractors into your house.

At first, you're all thrilled, because the lights start to work properly, and the plumbing works perfectly, and you don't snag your socks on the splintered floors, because all that's been smoothed out, and everything is hunky-dory.

When the Holy Spirit starts knocking out the walls, and pulling down the roof, that's when you freak out.

The White Mass is a powerhouse vehicle for the manifestation of God's will on earth.

You say the prayer and you eat the bread, and that is one thing.

But when you drink that strange wine, you write God a blank check, and you sign it in blood.

Steamboat Gothic

Steamboat Gothic is a style of architectural design. It was popular with rich steamboat captains who built lavish family houses in the 1800's. They are most prevalent along the Mississippi River, and the idea was to build the house to look as much as possible like your own steamboat. If the Delta Queen, or the Columbia on the Rivers of America ride at Disneyland, pop to mind, it's because they are classic examples of American river steamboats.

The best example in theater is the steamboat from Show Boat.

Critics say these old house are silly, fussy, and frilly, but these houses have more fans than their critics do, and far fewer detractors.

In their day there was serious competition between steamboat captains to outdo each other with details like gingerbread trim, brass doorknobs and fixtures, and even steamboat chimneys with the crown-shaped top that simulated the explosions so frequent to those early boilers.

Sonoma has one house that is Steamboat Gothic. It is located on a small patch of its original property at East Napa Street and Fifth Street East. You have to go into the Ledson development to see it, and although there are a lot of big "new" Victorian houses built around it, you can't help but notice the difference. It is called The Armstrong Place by long-time locals, and Armstrong Mansion by most people nowadays.

It was originally the Charles Van Damme House, after its Captain.

Mr. Ledson bought the original house on the original land, and then split up the property around the house into little squares, and put up big houses all around the main house. Add a grocery store, and a post office, and you can call it Ledsonville. As large and as lovely as the new houses are, the lots on which they sit are small.

The most polite thing that can be said is that the houses are spacious on the inside and handsome on the outside, and that the architect did a fine job combining classic Victorian features with the modern lifestyle of the California upper-middle class. What bothers me about them, although I'm sure they would be fun to live in provided one had a housekeeper and a gardener, is that I can't kick the overall impression that, expensive as they were to build, the layout betrays, at best, a trailer park mentality.

The same thing bothers me about the Ledson Winery out on Highway 12. It has the best materials, the most expensive marble, the most beautifully crafted woods and tiles, and it visibly aches to be a European castle. Bill Taylor, who grew up in the Donner House, dubbed it "The Monstrosity".

It makes a macabre impression, but that's not what bothers me.

What bothers me is that the Ledson Winery castle is like Toon Town in Disneyland. Everything is bloated. It's almost tragic. All that money, all that effort, all those exquisite materials, and all the talent that went into putting a fabulous European castle together, and it fails. It doesn't just fail; it fails dismally.

You step into the building, and you have to ask yourself, did this guy ever actually go to Europe? It's loud and gauche in an "Ugly American" way. It completely missed the mark.

You can't have elegance without restraint.

On my way to the radio station last night for my Strange Wine broadcast, I drove South, down First Street East, past the Sebastiani Theatre, and glanced over at the Ledson Hotel.

The groomsmen from a formal after-six wedding were out in front of the hotel in black ties and evening clothes. They were tall clean-cut young men of the White Anglo Saxon Protestant Persuasion, and they were handsome in a thin pale close-to-the-bone way. They were laughing, and obviously enjoying themselves after a busy Saturday night of pleasure and recreation.

But for all of that, they looked like morticians on a smoke break.

Katherine and Kyle Saint John invited me to a roommate interview dinner at the Armstrong House in the late eighties. I lived on France Street at the time, and the owner, Mr. Hummel, had just raised my rent from Sonoma Passport Economy status to Newcomer Luxury status, so I was on the hunt for a Sonoma Passport deal.

Not that I had anything against Mr. Hummel. He is one of the few people in my life who ever worried about my having enough to eat. Mr. Hummel was a retired Naval officer. He ran a tight ship, and I can respect that, but he expected me to be Mary Tyler Moore, which is about as far as anyone can get from being Carla Heine.

He came by to visit me one afternoon, and in a reflex reaction of which I myself have been guilty in the homes of others, he opened my refrigerator to inspect the contents. It was 1978, and I had recently closed Executive Search in San Francisco, and living within the local Sonoma economy was a challenge to which I had not yet adjusted.

So, the fridge was empty. I don't mean merely empty, but really empty. There were no contents at all to inspect in there. It was clean, yes, but as empty as it had been when it first hit the showroom floor in 1958.

"What is wrong with you?" Mr. Hummel said, obviously vexed by the discrepancy between what he expected to see and what he did not see. "You get some food in there, young lady. I will come back in one week, and when I do, I expect to see a refrigerator full of food. Do I make myself clear? Get some food in here."

A week later Mr. Hummel was back. He sauntered up to the door of the fridge and opened it. There he saw fat lush grapes in green, red and blue bunches. Large red apples rounded to perfection. Thick generous wedges of cheeses; Swiss, cheddar, and Monterey Jack. Rich rounds of whole grain breads. Big bright oranges, and thick bushy clumps of bright green broccoli. A picture perfect hamburger "with everything" waited invitingly next to a generous serving of French fries, and a big slice of Vanilla-frosted chocolate cake waited plumply on a white doily.

Mr. Hummel's eyes lingered on the fat rim around a roasted leg of mutton.

"That's better." he growled, and shut the door. After he left I opened the fridge and tossed every single item into a big brown cardboard box clearly labeled in think black permanent marker: "Shakespeare Feast - Plastic Foods". The fridge was as it had always been; as clean and as empty as the first day it rolled off the assembly line.

Hamlet was right when he said; "The play's the thing".

Katherine Saint John rented the Armstrong House for $1500.00 a month, and she figured $500.00 each would be a good deal for three people, and she was right. That's a Sonoma Passport price.

Katherine used to go with my brother Eric. She had been a guest at our parents' house, and she figured I was a good risk, and a safe bet, because I grew up in a haunted house, so the Armstrong House should pose no problem for someone like me.

People think that just because you grew up in a haunted house, haunted houses, and their unearthly occupants, will not bother you.

Nothing could be further from the truth. People think growing up in a haunted house is all one big jolly old picnic outing.

Horse feathers! Cow pies! Bull shit.

If you go to any of the Twelve-Step programs, and you live in Sonoma, it is better to go to Napa, Petaluma, or Santa Rosa. Marin County would be best, because chances are you wouldn't meet anyone at all from Sonoma, but Marin County is another planet, and they have otherworldly issues.

In Sonoma, there is no Anonymous in Alcoholics Anonymous, or in any of the other Anonymous programs. Which is fine, if that doesn't bother you.

It bothers me.

After Michael got hit on the head with the white light and left me for the new Magdalena Regime, I went to CODA (Co-Dependants Anonymous) in Napa. Just to keep my head on straight, so I wouldn't kill him. Or her. Or him and her.

There is a quiet but pronounced distain in Sonoma for Napa. For one thing, Napa never lost its port. For another, Napa got State money for their Asylum for the Criminally Insane before we got Federal money for our asylum. And, for another, their wines got popular before our wines got popular.

Sonoma Twelve Steppers go to Petaluma, or Santa Rosa to protect their privacy, but Napa is best. In Napa you are least apt to run into someone you've slept with.

CODA is good for anything. I used to rotate my addictions, and CODA gets to the root causes of addiction fastest, without focusing on any one particular substance, or habit. But you would be amazed at the number of people in the Napa CODA group who grew up in haunted houses.

Their childhood experiences make mine look like skim milk by comparison.

They came home from school to big maroon blood puddles seeping across Mother's clean linoleum kitchen floor; severed gibbering heads in linen closets full of white towels and ironed sheets; middle of the night screams, and pleas of little ghost children who cried, and begged their daddies not to cut off any more fingers.

It was October when I drove over to Kate and Kyle's for the interview dinner. The carriage drive was dirt and gravel then, just one wide strip of road that lead straight up to the front door. There was a strong wind that night, and it whistled through the holes in the shell of my Love Bug.

A warped brown leaf the size of a small pizza caught the gravel with its veined points, and clawed the ground against the wind. It lost the battle and sulkily crabbed its way across the road, four feet away from my front bumper.

When its low underbelly caught the headlamp light, it glowed a rotten pumpkin orange.

Not a good sign.

Dinner with Kyle and Katherine was lovely. The house looked the way the insidious ones always look; great. Five hundred dollars a month sounded great. The insidious ones usually have prices that sound great.

The water tower out at the Eldridge farm was only $80.00 a month, and that was in 2007. It looked great. It looked darling! It's 2008 now, over a year later and the price has gone down to $65.00 a month.

Don't go there.

After dinner Kate and Kyle took me on an extensive tour of the house. It was the first time I had ever set foot inside the Armstrong House. The first, and last time I ever did, or ever will, cross that threshold.

The downstairs rooms are public rooms. Kitchen, pantry, dining room, breakfast room, drawing room, parlors. Even the breakfast nooks have breakfast nooks in this house.

Nothing bad there. Great wood floors; high walls and ceilings. Classic.

The bedrooms and bathrooms for the family are on the second floor. The only safe bedroom is the one in the very front, the one that looks out over the old aviary, and onto the only road out.

All the servants' quarters were on the top floor, and they were tiny, stale, miserable little holes in the dark. All of them. They swallowed electric light. They had phantom smells of sickness, madness, and death. I was OK in the hallway. It was busy, busy, busy, because all the phantoms were in a hurry. They had places to go, and things to do. No time! No time!

I worked hard to keep my senses focused on what I saw with my eyes, and I willed myself not to be overwhelmed by the otherworldly pandemonium.

I was so proud of myself for coping so well under such adverse circumstances. There had been an inner knowledge that this was not going to be my next place of residence. Call it a foregone conclusion. Yet the desire to see the inside of the house was impossible to resist.

That's how these places get you; by the short and curly hairs of your curiosity. And a person can put up with a lot, even roommates, even phantom roommates, for only $500.00 a month. Up there on the top floor with all the dead servants in their eternally fearful dashings to and fro, my ego took center stage, and my mind basked happily in the reflected illusion of my calm self-control and my psychic greatness.

202

Pride. Pride, man. Pride. And vanity.

Puffed up with self-confidence I stepped over the narrow threshold, and into one of the little wall-flowered maid's rooms.

Pow! It hits me like a mud tidal wave. I look heavenward instinctively, for divine help. Slam! The ceiling drops and stops, four inches above my face. All I can see are two small slippered feet, a circular ruffle of dingy petticoat, another ruffle of dusty skirt, and two sets of knuckles above dirty fingernails.

Then the room starts to spin, and spin, and spin. It spins, and this poor girl hangs there eternally stuck between heaven and Hell from an old piece of dust- drenched rope she drug up from the basement.

Inside her, the Captain's unborn baby dies.

There is no such thing as an ex-smoker. If you never smoked, or you are really done with tobacco, and you never even get the urge, then you are not an ex-smoker; you are a real, honest-to-goodness, non-smoker. The rest of us are smokers who are not smoking at the moment.

All it takes for us to pick up a cigarette, and smoke it, is a push. It could be a push as small and as distant half-forgotten memory, or the upward curve in the corner of a smile, or a twinkle in the eye of that babe at the end of the bar. Or it could be a push as big as the explosion of a 747 airliner crashing into a New York skyscraper.

We are like diamonds. The most impenetrable known substance on earth. But there is a fault line in each of us that is ultimately and uniquely our own. Pound on that spot; whack it with all your might on one diamond, and nothing happens. Tap ever so gently on that spot with another diamond, and without a sound, the crack slides down the middle, and half the rock lets go.

It was a good cigarette. The first cigarette in five years, and the last cigarette for another five years. I smoked it slowly, soothingly, as I stood on the edge of the wide porch deck, balancing my body against the long high post of the balustrade. The red-fire tip at the end of the cigarette trembled brightly in the dark half-light of the incoming tulle fog. Kyle smoked. He had made me an offer that, under the circumstances, I could not refuse.

One of the loveliest sights in Sonoma, one of the eeriest, and most memorable sights in Sonoma, is the Steamboat Gothic house of Captain Charles Van Damme as it floats against the late night current above three feet of thick fresh-water tulle fog.

The soft lazy glow of interior lamps behind the windows cast waves of light and shadow as far as the distance between one shore and another, on a timeless river of silent grandeur. It is a sight that makes me stop, and stare every time I see it. I have seen it now for over forty years.

It never looses its impact.

That was the first and only time I have ridden aboard her on the sea of fog.

Once in a lifetime is enough to last me forever.

Intellectually, I knew the history of the house as well, if not better, than anyone in town. Intellectually, as I drove up the carriage walk, and slowed the Love Bug to let the pumpkin leaf crab its right of way across the dirt road, all the information was there in my head, right between my ears.

But once I crossed the threshold, and entered the house itself, the constant effort of being brave obscured my knowledge of why the house was haunted in the first place, and, in the second place, why it took so much effort to be there.

There is a reference to the Armstrong House in the diaries of the sisters who lived and taught at the Saint Joseph's Presentation Convent on West Napa Street at Third where the main building of Saint Francis School stands today.

The nuns used to walk the children of the Armstrong home after school. The children arrived early in the morning by carriage from the house, but those eight blocks, especially in those times, were too far for children to walk without an adult escort. In the diaries, one sister of the Presentation Convent wrote that they were "afraid to touch the gate of that house, for fear of soiling their souls and having to go again to confession".

There were "goings on" in that house.

They never got a sidewalk they didn't pay for themselves.

Captain Armstrong had been a worldly man. He drank brandy. He smoked cigars in the presence of his wife. He had no respect for women. He hosted wild parties, and the lights burned on well after ten o'clock, and even after midnight, and sometimes even on and on into the early hours of the morning.

Charles Van Damme had built the house far from town, so there would be no breach of his privacy, and no gossip. But there was gossip, and plenty of it. His wife, and later Captain Armstrong's wife were slandered in private, and shunned in public.

In her loneliness, her isolation, and her shame, Mrs. Armstrong became a laudanum addict. Her husband deflowered one of the maids; the maid became pregnant and, thus ruined, she hung herself in her dark little room upstairs.

Their only son, equally uninvited and shunned in Sonoma, sought friends and entertainment in Napa, and on his return home one foggy night, lost control of the horses that drew the family carriage as he crossed the river.

He fell beneath the wheels, and died.

My mother, Elizabeth, told me that the next owners of the house also had an only son, and that he also did his partying in Napa. She told me that he was crossing the same river in the same place in his car, when he lost control of the vehicle, was thrown from the car, and died. I don't know if that's true.

The real steamboat, The Charles Van Damme, took cars and buggies, and horses from Sausalito to San Francisco before the Golden Gate Bridge was built. They gave night passengers little paper containers with a toothbrush and toothpaste.

The Charles Van Damme was scuttled in Sausalito at Gate Five Road. Juanita lived in it and ran a restaurant in it until it was fireswept. She had so many animals on board that it was nicknamed "The Ark".

All that is left of The Charles Van Damme today is her paddle wheel.

CHARLES VAN DAMME

THE FERRYBOAT COMMEMORATIVE PROJECT.

*Keeping Her Creative Spirit alive
by Telling Her Story, Creating a Monument,
Replacing the Cultural Center that She once provided.*

The Asylum At Eldridge

My usual arrangement with Twilight Tour guests who are psychics is simple. I let them go first. They tell me what they pick-up at our various stops, then I tell them what I know of the history, and reputation of the building, or location.

I didn't know Prem and Jason were psychic when I met them, and the more I think about what it means to be "psychic" the more I think Prem and Jason are not so much "psychic" as "awake". Awake about who they are, where they are, and what they see, and hear around them.

Jason and Prem planned to sleep over at a lady-friend's house on the starry night we went out in Lola. The lady-friend got off work late, and Jason and Prem wanted to go get her, and take her with us to see the insane asylum at Eldridge half a mile North of her house.

I was game.

When we got there I was amazed and delighted to discover their friend was one of my favorite former Saint Francis parents. Her beautiful, funny, talented daughter was all grown up now.

"Miss Heine!" she squealed happily as she hugged me tightly, eyes bright with joy. "I can't believe these guys found you!"

"We found each other!" I explained merrily.

There was a great deal of cheerful fussing, and sweater trading, and jacket changing. It was Christmas in July. Cold fog had engulfed The Valley. Outside her house our hot breath formed solid streams from our mouths and our ruddy-pink nostrils. Dragon's breath at Chinese New Year.

They laughed, tumbled into Lola, and we rolled out into the night.

Eldridge is officially a town, but it isn't a real town. It has census data on the Internet like a real town, a post office, a credit union for banking, a fire department, a police department, and a cemetery whose shameful history is a grotesquerie. Eldridge even has its own zip code. There is also an animal farm, and an old dairy.

The animal farm is a great place to visit with children because it is a community outreach area, which means they want people from the outside to come in and see the animal farm, so it is very visitor friendly, and you won't see any of the patients because they are not allowed to work there anymore.

The residents at Eldridge used to do light work on the farm, but the State decided that it was forced labor, and that isn't legal, though they got paid, but it wasn't anywhere near minimum wage, so that isn't legal either. Prisoners at San Quentin who work in the kitchen make $30.00 a month. Chinese coolie wages. Anyway, now, instead of going along the old walks, and taking care of the bunnies, and the chickens, and raising vegetables, the residents have to stay inside, watch TV, and act like vegetables.

I have negative judgments about that.

The good news is that you can drive into Eldridge, and at the four-way stop where the Indian used to sit and wave to each passer-by, you can go East, drive away from the original Victorian brick building and the American Flag, and go up the hill to what they call the Junior Farm.

The Junior Farm actually has a summer day camp program now, but you can visit any time, and bring as many people as you like, and even bring a picnic lunch. The barn is long, and low, and full of stalls.

They have barn cats and barn kittens, roosters, chickens, tons of guinea pigs, real pot-bellied pigs, chinchillas who take twirly-dry dust-baths in clear round glass volcano-ash tubs. They have wild turkeys, llamas, ponies, donkeys, peacocks, peahens, miniature horses, and oodles and oodles of bunnies.

No rats.

They used to raise white albino lab rats at Eldridge in highly controlled colonies. They were huge, and sometimes weighed five to eight pounds. That's the size of a big Foster Farms roasting chicken. The babies are really cute, once you get past their tail, which is prehensile like a monkey tail and looks very reptilian. Kindness takes over, and they become quite loveable.

These special laboratory rats were practically impossible to get. They were specially bred, if not genetically altered, and unlike pet-store rats who live about two years, the Eldridge lab rats had life spans of eight to ten years.

These giant rats were really important to the research scientists, and unless you knew a dad who worked "out there", and who would smuggle one of them out illegally for you, you could live in Sonoma your whole life, and never even see a mutant Eldridge lab rat.

Sadly, when the experimental human population began to die off, they killed off the experimental rat colonies, too. A friend of a friend snuck one of the Eldridge rats out as a pet for his son. That went over like a lead balloon.

The boy was dead scared of her on sight, so she came to live with me. Ikura, I named her, because she had ruby-pink salmon-egg eyes.

Smart, Ikura. Spooky smart.

The rat colonies are gone now, but the vast fields of empty weeds with horses, turkeys, barns, and almost equally vast fields of neat lush lawns with sprinklers, baseball diamonds, and night lighting are all still right there.

There are many large quasi-modern post-war buildings that look like indifferently constructed WPA projects, good enough for government work, as well as a number of long low dormitory buildings, and a series of two and three bedroom houses for resident doctors. Eldridge has a stated resident population of 1200 souls. The population dwindles daily.

Eldridge also has its own dental facility, medical facility, morgue, mortuary, crematorium, and graveyard. Len Dillman's dad worked in the motor pool.

The State talks about turning it into part of the University of California system someday. If they do, they ought to have one groundbreaking parapsychology department.

The CIA did a lot of work with pharmaceutical LSD out there. And intravenous radioactive liquids. A surprising amount of the LSD made it out onto the streets of Sonoma in the 1960's and 1970's. We are not talking about the little cartoon blotter acid cut with arsenic and speed, which they sell nowadays in Sonoma, and which contains only 80 to 85 micrograms of lysergic acid diethylamide. Oh, no!

We are talking about standard dosages of gelatin capsules containing five to ten thousand micrograms each.

Hey, Aldous Huxley, hold onto your Tibetan Book of The Dead!

It was my next-door neighbor Dr. Taylor who first told me the story of Eldridge. I was 12, and his daughter Lorraine had not yet begun to hate my guts. Dr. Taylor was the dentist out there. In Sonoma Speak Eldridge is "Out There". El Verano is "Over There" and anything South of where you are standing is "Down There". That way you don't have to sully your tongue.

Dr. Taylor's secret philanthropic contribution to the Sonoma community was that, if you needed dental work, and could not afford to have it done elsewhere, he would take you "out there" at night, and fix your teeth for no money at all.

Dr. Taylor never had to worry about freeloaders, because going out there was seriously creepy, and you had to be truly desperate to ask him for help.

People in Sonoma would take second jobs to pay for their dental work just to avoid having to go "Out There", especially at night.

Dr. Taylor was a slim man, light boned and pleasant to talk to, but myopic. He wore glasses, but that had nothing to do with his tunnel vision. Over the decades it's been my experience that however broad their other interests may be, dentists have to focus constantly on this tiny little area of one tooth, so perhaps myopia is not an accurate metaphor.

Perhaps "extremely focused" is closer to the tooth.

When Dr. Taylor told me the story of the Philadelphia Experiment it sounded perfectly logical. Eddie and I learned about Tessla's murder, and the confiscation of Tessla's electro-static coil and his research papers, and Professor Einstein's equation of special relativity and his time-space theories, in fourth grade at the Bell Lane School.

So it made sense to me that someone really smart could put them together and come up with a way of making a battleship disappear in the middle of Philadelphia Harbor. Consider what they did with the Atom Bomb. The only part that didn't make sense was the part about using human beings. Guinea pigs are so cheap.

Forty-five people out of a skeleton crew of 600 survived. That is still a major miracle when you add the fact that these men were exposed to six times the amount of radiation that is fatal to human beings.

Professor Einstein wrote a three-page handwritten letter pleading with the President not to try it with people. But Germany was making inroads with heavy water. That was one of Eddie's favorite topics in fourth grade.

All's fair in love and war. Right? Death and taxes. Right? Lead, follow, or get out of the way. Right?

If you are not up on the Philadelphia Experiment, it was a government cover-up from the days before the American government got really good at covering up. They wanted a way to make their war ships invisible.

Invisibility was an edge that would surely win World War II for the US, if it got off the drawing board in time. Typical of governmental thinking, rather than just bend a thin layer of space around the battleship, they moved the entire SS Eldridge and her crew 300 miles away via another dimension, and killed almost everyone.

Men came back fused to the bulkhead walls. Dead. Dying. And worse.

They used a tank to kill a mosquito.

Actually, they ended up killing 555 people. But they told the families of all 600 men that their loved ones had died in the line of duty. Families were given their flags, their benefits, and told to move on with their lives.

Meanwhile, the 45 survivors were on a bus being shipped out for incarceration in a three-story Victorian brick asylum out in the middle of nowhere, which turned out to be in Sonoma Valley, California.

When that B movie, "The Philadelphia Experiment", came out of Hollywood, Dr. Taylor's story came back to me. Not that Eldridge had never entirely left my mind. It never does. Not entirely.

Mr. Smith, my chemistry teacher at Sonoma Valley Union High, was an Eagle Scout leader. In the Spring of 1970, he formed a group for college-prep students who were also pre-med candidates, and he made us all official Eagle Scouts.

I was the only girl, but I'd always wanted to be an Eagle Scout.

Mr. Smith was sexy in an absent-minded-professor way. He took us out there one evening for a tour, and we met a really famous doctor who was in charge of the place at the time, but it was not Dr. Poindexter. This doctor took us to see the fetus collection, but not the radioactive brain collection.

That was off-limits. Way off limits.

The fetuses were in big glass specimen jars. Like the jar Captain Love used for the head of the man who was not Joaquin Murrieta, only instead of glass tops, these glass jars has black plastic screw-on tops. Probably Bakelite.

Plain unvarnished wood shelves covered the walls from the ground all the way up to the ceiling. Fetuses float in formaldehyde. These unborn babies were all legally harvested from the residents without their consent.

Dr. Taylor worked for Dr. Poindexter, and he said that after most of the Philadelphia Experiment survivors died, they moved the remaining men into the other wards, but when they tried to return the original patients to the big Victorian brick building, they found that they couldn't use the building anymore at all. Dr. Poindexter had to transfer his inmates back over to stay with the patients at the Napa Asylum for the Criminally Insane.

Is a change really as good as a rest?

The problem was that when the original patients got put back into the Sonoma Asylum, they couldn't stand to be in the building. They, and the nurses, got seasick and nauseous so quickly that they couldn't even make it the bathrooms to throw up; they had to use the wastepaper baskets.

And they saw the sailors, Dr. Taylor said, they saw the sailors walking right through the walls. That's why Dr. Poindexter had to evacuate his inmates immediately.

Things have to get pretty bad before the Napa Asylum For The Criminally Insane is an improvement.

Dr. Poindexter was understandably upset, and he wrote a strong letter to Washington DC and told them all about it. He said that they had ruined his building; he wanted them to replace the entire structure. He wanted them to replace it and he wanted them to pay for it, too.

They said, "No."

Dr. Poindexter wrote again.

Again they said, "No."

When he wrote the third time, Dr. Poindexter told them that if they didn't give him the money to replace the building which they had permanently ruined, he would go to the newspapers and magazines, and tell them about the 45 survivors, and how their wives, and parents, and children had all been lied to by the government.

Dr. Poindexter threatened to tell the press that these citizens' husbands, sons, brothers, and fathers were still alive when the government pronounced them dead, and these families had been denied their last chance to see these men while they were still alive.

That worked.

That worked so brilliantly that Dr. Poindexter got thirteen million dollars the first time he used that technique, and another six million dollars the second time. Eldridge was the first State facility to have all electric cars and people movers.

As the biggest State Hospital in the system, over 5,000 people were involuntarily sterilized there. Abortions were performed there regularly, and secret government experiments were conducted there, too. The US government got their money's worth out there, believe me.

The Nazis weren't the only ones working with twins.

High-ranking government officials occasionally misused their rank to send their pregnant daughters there to give birth out of wedlock, and the babies were entered into the mainstream "patient" population.

Sonoma did what Sonoma does best; Sonoma kept its collective mouth shut. Eldridge money put a lot of bread and butter on a lot of Sonoma tables.

Eldridge was the single largest employer in all of Sonoma County.

"Specimen Number Such and Such" was how they labeled patients. Their ashes were buried in the mass graves at the cemetery out there, unless the family came to get them, and even then their brains remained in what is probably the most extensive radioactive brain collection in the world today.

Patients who were pregnant when they arrived for sterilization had often carried their babies almost to term, and these babies were removed, and added to the collection of fetuses in specimen jars, just like the brains.

Some babies were badly deformed, and some looked normal, if you can call a dead baby in a glass jar full of formaldehyde normal. The glass specimen jars were 12 inches in diameter, reminiscent of the bedside water-jar that contained the head of my great great-grandfather's best friend.

None of us openly freaked out, or threw up. We were too busy trying to act cool, failing to look cool, and simultaneously trying to see as much of the collection as we could wrap our brains around.

Eldridge was Sonoma State Hospital when we were there. When Sonoma State University opened, people used to snicker when they heard the words "Sonoma State". Modern as it was for its time, we could easily imagine the wards, which we never got to tour. Jack London was inspired to write a short story after his visit to Sonoma Asylum for the Feeble Minded. I'm surprised he didn't write a book!

Mr. London entitled his tale "Told in The Drooling Ward" and interestingly enough, it is written in the first person.

Here is how it starts:

"Me? I'm not a drooler. I'm the assistant. I don't know what Miss Jones or Miss Kelsey could do without me. There are fifty-five low-grade droolers in this ward. How could they ever all be fed if I wasn't around? I like to feed droolers. They don't make trouble. They can't. Something's wrong with most of their legs and arms, and they can't talk. They're very low-grade. I can walk, and talk, and do things. You must be careful with the droolers and not feed them too fast. Then they choke. Miss Jones says I'm an expert. When a new nurse comes I show her how to do it. It's funny watching a new nurse try to feed them. She goes at it so slow and careful that suppertime would be around before she finished shoving down their breakfast. Then I show her, because I'm an expert. Dr. Dalrymple says I am, and he ought to know. A drooler can eat twice as fast if you know how to make him."

No wonder the respectable Sonoma society ladies were appalled by Jack London. Calling him "The Hero of the Common Man" was not a compliment. It endeared him to none, but the common. In Sonoma society, it was a cutting remark.

One of my Twilight Tour ladies was a nurse out there, at Eldridge, for over 40 years. When we were there, in Lola, she told me that the fetus collection was still the last step in the hiring process.

"We take them in there after the interviews." she said. "And if they so much as bat an eyelash, they are back out on the street looking for work. Still, the original building was much worst on everybody.

"We only used it to store files. When the doctors needed a the files, they would send a nurse in to get it from the cabinets, but too often they came back empty handed. Then they tried to send us in there two by two, but all that did was waste two people's time. They always came back empty handed."

"What was their excuse?" I asked her. I liked her. She is built like a bird with tight curls and an all-natural salt and pepper hairdo. She is a no-nonsense gal who has the forthright manner I associate with schoolteachers, secretaries, nurses and other pink-collar women who pioneered the workplace, and blazed the trail for the rest of us. "They had to say something to the doctors who sent them for the files." I added, as an addendum.

"No, they didn't." she says confidently. "It happened so often, everybody knew that once you got into the building, you just plumb forgot. They finally had to move the files to another building."

"What about Chamberlain Hall?" I asked, casually, so as not to sound too eager and put her off. Chamberlain Hall is a touchy subject in Sonoma because the operating rooms, and the mortuary are in Chamberlain Hall.

Sterilizations. Abortions. Brain harvests.

"We lost a lot of night watchmen in Chamberlain Hall." she says. "They'd come in the day after their first night, to pick up their checks, and to say they wouldn't be back."

"What was their excuse?"

"Most didn't give one. You'd just look at their face, and you'd know. Some saw The Red Ball, some saw the ghosts of the children who play with The Red Ball, and some saw Other Things. It's where the operating rooms, and the morgue are. Many of the patients didn't know what was happening to them when they were taken there, because they were retarded, you see."

I saw.

"It must have been terrible for them, not to understand, not to be able to defend themselves." I said. "Were the ghostly children patients?"

"No." she says, and nods, quick, like a bird. "They were the children of one of the doctors. He used to bring them with him on the weekends, when he came in to work in his office, and they'd play in the hallways with the red ball. Some of our workers saw the ghosts of the children in the hall, but some just saw The Red Ball. Actually," she confided, "It was worst when it was just The Red Ball. Especially at night. At least when the ghosts of the children were there, The Red Ball made some sort of sense. But all by itself, it made no sense at all."

"What did it do?" I asked her.

"It bounced." she says ominously.

"I figured that." I said with good humor. "But that's not enough to scare a grown man off a job with good pay, a pension program, and full benefits."

"It is when the ball bounces up the stairs behind you, or follows you down the halls, or just floats down the hallway behind you two feet above the ground."

Her point was well taken.

"Whoa!" said Jason when he first saw the original asylum building. "Look at all the German Shepards."

"And the armed guards." says Prem, nodding.

"And the sailors playing cards." says Jason.

So I look, and thanks to their amplification, I see all that, but I also see the funniest thing. Yes, I saw the guards, and yes, they were armed, on patrol, marching around the buildings, but there was a never-ending parade of German Shepards. Four abreast, all on leashes that went up into thin air.

It was a merry-go-round of dogs making a big circle around the building; big, buff, healthy full-grown German Shepards. They looked serious, too. Hard working dogs. Not pets. There must have been a thousand of them.

I laughed out loud.

"I don't believe this!" I said. "I don't believe there were ever this many German Shepards in one place anywhere, ever, Jason, not even in Germany in 1941."

"Look again." says Jason, and I look again, and ok, ok, this is better. It isn't tons and tons of German Shepards patrolling the building like some canine carousel of a hundreds and one German Shepards; it was the same dogs going around, and around, over and over again

There is a video on You Tube, if you want to see a video of a paranormal investigation that took place out there. HPI from Sacramento is an international group of paranormal investigators that did a field investigation and a man named Face, from Off The Hook TV, filmed the HPI research excursion to Eldridge.

Face did a lot of the camera work for a movie called "Jackass" which may, or may not be a recommendation. He wasn't responsible for the content.

The video's funny. Not just funny, amusing, but funny, peculiar and weird.

Face got a really, really weird bunch of EVP sounds, and the photographers got all kinds of orb photographs. And the tick-tick-tick of the Geiger counter makes me think this buildings' reputation may have less to do with the paranormal, and more to do with extreme radiation poisoning.

After all, Uranium-239 has a half-life of 239 years.

HPI also brought electronic voice pattern equipment, magnetic resonance meters, and Paul Dale Roberts. Paul is a big name in paranormal journalism on the Internet. Google his name and wow! He wrote an article about that HPI investigation and you can read it on the Internet, too.

My fully charged camera battery drained dead just after our arrival. We picked up a wide variety of phantom smells there, too. I got a few good shots, and when I got a chance to view them, there were definite orbs in my photographs.

People say these are just dust reflected back in the images by the light from the flash, but my flash died first, before I took my pictures, so that explanation cuts no ice with me. Since that trip the orbs are in a good ten percent of my digital photos, with or without flash power.

"She's trying to climb out." Prem says by the window on the ground level off to the left of the front of the building. "Poor thing! She's trying to escape through the laundry room window. They keep catching her, and bringing her back. She can't get away. She keeps on trying to get out, and they keep catching her, and bringing her back! Poor thing."

"That's only an imprint, Prem." Jason tells her. "What worries me is this big black dragon climbing up the building. This thing is Evil."

Even though I stood only five feet from Jason, all I could see was a black spiral of darkness. The kind that comes out of those charcoal pellets they give you at Fourth of July. You light them on the pavement, and they curl up like a black foam snake, but I couldn't see Jason's Evil dragon.

Fine by me.

The Indians told the white people not to build there. They said it was an Evil place, where Evil things came out of a hole in the ground. There was a spring there, and there were rituals the Indians preformed there, and it is right across The Sacred Valley from the big Indian cave behind the 85-foot waterfall on the Bouverie Audubon Preserve.

Right about the time Ishi was at Berkeley, a lone Indian came out of the woods and walked down across the property. He told the white men it was alright for them to live there, and even build their houses there, but under no circumstances were they to dig in that cave, because the cave was where they buried their dead, and it is wrong to disturb the dead.

Go on an Audubon tour there, and a guide will take you to the cave. It is the length of two limousines, and just as deep. It is right behind the first of three waterfalls up there. It is 85 feet from the top of the first waterfall to the huge pool below. Irene Cunha's ex-boyfriend is the only person who ever took that fall and lived to talk about it. He was taken out of there in a helicopter.

Don't go alone. Too dangerous. Last time I went up there a six foot long rattlesnake crossed our path on the trail, and my guide, who was not an Audubon guide, but an employee of Mr. Bouverie, shot it and cut off the head, and buried the head off the trail, so nobody would step on it, and get accidently venomized.

We went up to swim in the big deep basalt pools under the waterfalls. Ice cold. Twenty feet deep. Pencil dive, and you feel like you will never get back up to the surface before you freeze to death.

I know this from personal experience.

The black snaky whatever-it-was I saw, that Jason saw as an Evil dragon, was about three feet thick, and twenty feet long. It curled a third of the way up the building. It smelled bad, too.

They used to say that although two Indian men could bring in the big bear for The Bear Sacrifice, it took 12 men to bring in a Sonoma Valley rattlesnake, for the Rattlesnake Sacrifice.

When I first heard this, I believed two men could bring in a bear, because bears in Sonoma were totally tame.

Bears were treated with religious awe, and they walked among the Indians in The Sacred Valley like men. In fact, the Indians believed that the bear was a man, but he did something to anger The Creators, so The Creators turned him into a bear-man as punishment.

Bear meat is taboo as a food source, so as not to interfere between the bear's misdeed, and The Creators' punishment. Later I learned that two men could bring in a bear because they took turns wearing the bear out, by double-teaming him.

When they told me it took 12 Indians to bring in one rattlesnake, I thought they were joking. I thought: 'What a bunch of sissy Indians! I could bring in a rattlesnake with nothing but a long stiff pole and a thin rope!'

Did you know that the average rattlesnake in Sonoma today is between two and three feet long? They have gotten much smaller, and they have started to breed without rattles. I found a three foot long one out in the parking lot under my Lola. It took the Animal Control people three hours to catch it. And they are experts, with state of the art equipment made specifically for catching rattlesnakes. They took it away for re-release up on Rattlesnake Ridge.

So my theory about being able to bring one in with a pole and a rope was, how can I put this compassionately? Ignorant? Arrogant? Stupid?

Two hundred years ago when the Spanish arrived in Sonoma with the gunpowder and bullets that made steel armor and the arrow obsolete, the average size of a rattlesnake was 22 feet long and three feet thick. That is why it took 12 men to bring one in for sacrifice. Not only were they way too wily for double-teaming, but can you imagine the size of their venom-pouches and their fangs?

The black snake I saw in front of Jason was about that size.

Was the Sonoma asylum at Eldridge built on top of the sacred Indian rattlesnake worship site? The rattlesnake and the bear were counterpoint guardians of the Other World. Nobody got to speak to the dead without going through either the Bear Spirit, or the Rattlesnake Spirit.

The Rattlesnake Spirit's job in Sonoma Valley was similar to the Bear Spirit's job. He was a guardian spirit of the underworld, but he was not like the Bear. If you had a problem, first you went to the Bear Spirit. But if the Bear Spirit could not help you, or refused to help you, and you would not take "No" for an answer, you could go to the Rattlesnake Spirit for help. It was the most dangerous path, and most apt to kill you, or drive you insane.

Oddly enough, I don't know anything else about the annual Rattlesnake Sacrifice. I don't know what moon it belonged to, or how it was done, or if they used the ChiCha, or not. The only thing I know is that it was like turning your back on God when He said "No" and asking the Devil instead.

The Indians warned the white men not to even go near this site, because bad spirits came out of the ground here. It is possible that the fumes from the geothermal vents under this site caused hallucinations along the same lines as those experienced by the Oracle at Delphi.

The white men who built the insane asylum there right must not have been aware that it is right on top of the Roger's Fault.

The Bear Sacrifice

Mark Oltz is a handsome fellow, with even features, a good clean jaw line, and a firm chin. His skin is ivory, and he's built like the kind of man you'd want to be with if some inebriated micro-brain with a mondo-chip on his shoulder got out of hand in the dark alley behind Steiner's Bar.

Mark is attractive and fun to be with, but despite his good looks and charm, the most attractive thing about Mark is his unique way of looking at the world, and his inimitable ability to communicate his way of seeing things around him to the world at large. Mark is the first person to film an underground Chinese tunnel in the town of Sonoma.

Mark and I met this past Summer in front of the Mission at nine o'clock on a clear cool Sonoma morning. Mark is the totally ingenious creative director and inspired video photographer behind NBC's show "In Wine Country".

We started in front of the three polished granite memorials slabs that run along First Street East beside the Mission.

Mark took digital images of the engraved dedication, and the little carved daisies, and then he started to read the 800 names.

"Are these in English, or Spanish?" he asked.

"Spanish, Latin, and Italian." I said. "These are the baptismal names of the Indians. They were not allowed to use their birth names."

"So where are the bodies, exactly?" asked Mark. "Under the memorial?"

"No, they are four feet down under the street."

"You mean under the bushes along the sidewalks?"

"No, but that's what people are supposed to think. They are four feet under the asphalt of First Street East itself, between the sidewalk curbs. We drive over them everyday on our way to Little League."

"But don't the Indian tribes get upset?" Mark asked.

"They used to get upset," I explained, "but since we put up the memorial, if they do get upset, they don't complain to us about it."

There were 1250 men, women, and children buried in this mass grave. They were neophytes, newly baptized into the Catholic faith, who died in the smallpox epidemic between 1837 and 1839.

We were only able to get 800 names from the baptismal records of the Mission. They keep those down in the San Diego Mission. Now that

234

the names we did get are written in stone, the official number of dead Indians under the asphalt is 800, not 1250.

We know better.

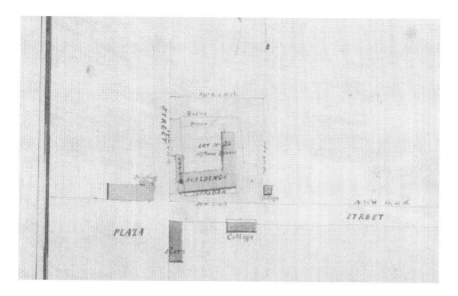

Tribal Elders from the Emerald Triangle, Mendocino, Trinity, and Humboldt counties where the reservations are, wrote to the Sonoma City Fathers for over 40 years asking "May we please have the bones of our dead?"

The Sonoma City Fathers wrote back and said: "No. You may not."

Eventually the Indians got tired of polite letters.

Finally they sent down 15 of their scruffiest Indians with plain white picket signs that simply said: 'Give us back the bones of our dead.'

"They vigiled from dusk until dawn by candlelight at night, and from sunrise until sunset; from Friday at sunset to Sunday at sunset." I told Mark. "The following Friday night they came back again, and by Saturday at noon the City had created a legally binding written compromise."

"What was the compromise?" Mark asked, looking at the little white daisies carved into the granite memorials that mark the names of Indian children.

"These three marble slabs. Plus a solemn promise to give them the back the bones of their dead. At some unspecified date in the future. We got as many names as we could from the baptismal records of the Sonoma Mission from the Mission San Diego. The records are kept there because the Indians burned this mission down seven times to free the female slaves."

"Why was that?"

"Sonoma padres kept the women shackled here behind the Mission walls mostly against their will. Much of the mission was made of wood, so it was highly flammable. Rescuing the women was their first priority. The men were shackled in Spanish iron on the ground floor of the adobe Barracks, which wasn't as flammable, across the street. They were impossible to free."

Spanish soldiers with guns were barracked on the second floor.

Sonoma was the center of the Indian slave trade. Indians either converted to Christianity, or they were captures and imprisoned, and sold for two dollars.

"Two Dollars?" Mark shook his head when I shared that little tid bit.

"Not much is it?" I said. "A good horse went for $1600.00 in those days. Down at the port, you could buy a 13 year old Chinese girl for only $13.00, so that shows you how low Indians sat on the economic value scale. Negro slaves in the south were worth $800.00 to 1400.00"

We walked to the back of the Sonoma Mission, behind the last adobe wall, and I showed Mark where the Bear Sacrifice took place. Half of the site belongs to the Castagnaso's family. The other half belongs to the State.

"They put the bear here, in a deep round pit, and they kept him drunk on Manzanita berry cider, and the Indian princesses brushed his fur with the spines of the sacred salmon, and fed him sacred honey, and fish, and berries.

The shamans and chieftains, many of whom were women, sat in a spiral around the Bear pit. When the ChiCha was ready to be fermented, they buried the ChiCha gourds in the dirt, and left them underground for 21 days while the maidens feasted the bear."

"What was the ChiCha made from?" Mark asks.

"Crushed corn, Amanita Mascaras mushroom, and saliva."

"Magic Mushrooms?"

"Yes. Magic mushrooms." I confirmed.

One-third magic mushroom, one-third crushed blue corn, and one-third saliva. It's the same recipe they used in Sumer, and Cuzco, but they use Amanita Panthera in South America, because the panther is the strongest animal on that continent. Here in North America it's the bear.

Mr. Yount, of the original Sebastopol, which became Yountville after his death, and six of his friends, had a contest one day, up where the white cross is outside the Mountain Cemetery. They placed big bets to see who among them could kill the most bears between sunrise and sunset. They took their rifles, and a barrel of brandy, and sat up there shooting passing bears all day. Mr. Yount won with a total of 153 bears, Then they went home.

They left the bodies there to rot.

If seven men shoot 100 bears, that is 700 bears, plus Mr. Yount's extra 53 bears, equals 753 dead bears. And that is a conservative estimate, because at least one of his friends would have given Mr. Yount a run for his money. It is doubtful he beat them all by half a hundred bears. The actual total was probably close to 1,000 dead bears.

Poor bears. Some contest.

The place where the Bear Sacrifice took place on every October full moon for an estimated 80,000 years is an empty field at the moment, like I said, and it belongs to the Castagnaso Family.

The sidewalk there is new, because the old City Fathers knew what the land had been used for by the Indians, and since the original City Charter says they didn't have to pay to put one there, they didn't.

I don't know who paid for this one.

It's the same all along the Castagnaso's property on East Spain, because that was the old Mission Cemetery grounds, and Mr. Castagnaso promised The Church never to plant, or plow, when he bought the property. It wasn't a written agreement. Mr. Castagnaso was a man who could keep a promise based on his word, and a handshake.

Not like Some.

The City of Sonoma has entered into an agreement with the Castagnaso Family to take over the house, the farm, and the grounds. They plan to use the money from the low-income housing fund. Low income housing in Sonoma starts for incomes of $49,000.00 or less. Most of us are pleased with the arrangement, and willing to let go of our positions on raiding the low-income coffers to swing the deal. What those in the know are not saying is, the City can't afford to have anybody digging up those Mission graves. We have to buy it to keep the graves secret.

There were also no sidewalks all the way down East Second Street, South of Napa, because that was Prostitute Row before the Women's' League for Decency strong-armed the men into burning down the shanty town at the Embarcadero, droving the prostitutes to El Verano, and firesweeping all the Chinese tents and shacks in town to forcibly expelled the Chinese.

Horsewhips, fire, and gunpowder. That's what they used.

Ironic, isn't it? Since the Chinese invented gunpowder.

That must have been a night to remember. Or to try to forget.

ChiCha is so much a part of South American culture that it has descended to modern times, and it is a refreshing drink that can be made from scratch, or purchased in powder form. Of course, today they use water instead of saliva, no Amanita Panthera mushroom, and it has no alcohol. It is similar to the powdered American Cool-Aid beverage.

The sacred ritual ChiCha had to be fermented underground for 21 days and 21 nights. Seven was a sacred number to the Indians, because the Sky Canoe came from the constellation of the Seven Sisters.

After this three-week process, Indian Princesses of the highest rank kept the chosen bear drunk on Manzanita cider, served him wild honey and sweet berries, and fed him sacred salmon raised in the fishponds behind the Blue Wing Inn. They combed his fur with salmon spines, and buffed his claws with leather.

By the end of the 21 days the gourds of ChiCha were ready to be removed from the earth. The ChiCha was now a 14% alcoholic, and a seriously hallucinogenic psychotropic psycadellic.

On the night of the first full October moon the men assumed their positions in the sacred spiral at sunset and the ChiCha gourds were unearthed, their contents consumed, and then the Chief of Chiefs sacrificed the bear.

The Chief of Chiefs was really the King of the North American Indians this side of the Rocky Mountains, but the Indians weren't about to tell the Spaniards that was Sum Yet Ho.

Indian runners from Cuzco had already told the Sonoma Indians what the Spanish did to their Kings. Conversely, the Spanish would never designate Sum Yet Ho with so powerful and godlike a generational title themselves. Vallejo went so far as to call him Prince Sum Yet Ho, but that was as far as he went, and he went too far by half as far as most Sonoma Spaniards were concerned. After all the Pope decreed they had no souls, and with Indians going for $2.00 each, and what with Sonoma being the center of Indian slave trade, that was good enough for them.

It was the Chief of Chiefs' responsibility and privilege to kill the Bear, and remove his heart, and his eyes at the start of the Bear Sacrifice.

The Chief of Chiefs drank the heart's blood from the living heart of the bear, and swallowed the eyeballs of the Bear whole. In this way he gained the Bears' courage, and spirit, and he gained the Bear's vision; to see with the eyes of the Bear was Big Medicine.

Today in California the average size of a bear heart is about the size of a cantaloupe. Before European's arrived in Sonoma Valley with their guns, the average size of a bear heart was the size of a basketball.

If you can imagine a heart the size of a basketball, then you can imagine how much blood the Chief of Chief's drank from the living heart of the bear.

Once drained, the heart itself was passed around the spiral. Each person took one bite, and passed it on until it was completely consumed. Then the sacrificial Bear was skinned, and the Chief of Chiefs climbed into the bear's skin the way we would climb into a wet suit. His hands and feet went where the bear's paws had been. His head was inside the bear's scalp and face. Then the skin was sewn shut with sinew, and he began the three nights and three days of Bear Dance Ritual.

Joseph Campbell said the Bear Dance Ritual is the oldest religious ritual on Planet Earth. It predates both the Cro-Magnon and Neanderthal cultures. Professor Leaky found man-made tools in California that date back 75,000 years. He said snake worship historically comes in second, worldwide.

These observations do not contradict the arrival of other people from other cultures over the Bering Straits. It merely predates them by 55,000 years.

Ancient Indian chant songs tell of The Others who came over the top of the world 15,000 years ago, but they were not The First People who were put here by The Star People when the Sky Canoe landed behind where the Sonoma Mission stands today.

Men and women did not live together then as they do now. There were no issues about equality. Each gender had its own gifts, but women were superior. Women made the major decisions. Women were goddesses.

The whole area around the Bear pit was the mens' center in The Sacred Valley. During the Bear Sacrifice itself the Sacred Spiral spread out to include between 15,000 and 25,000 Chiefs and Shamans.

When the Franciscan Padres arrived in Sonoma and established the Mission San Francisco de Solano, they filled the bear pit with dirt and planted prickly-pear cactus over it, so the Indians couldn't even walk there anymore. The Indians were forbidded to even talk about it.

The women's area, with the hot sands they used to cure cramps and increase fertility, had huge hot springs that fed the birthing pools. There were also the burial grounds for mothers and babies lost in childbirth nearby. These were all where the Fairmont Sonoma Mission Inn Hotel and luxury Spa is today.

I find that serendipitous, don't you?

On the third night of the Bear Dance Ritual, the princesses and high caste women proceeded by torchlight from The Sacred Springs, and presented themselves to the Chief of Chiefs who was now one with the spirit of the Great Bear of Bears. They brought with them as an offering The Gift.

The Gift was what the Indians called the physical act of love, and it belonged to a woman, the same way a car, or a sweater belongs to us today. The Gift was theirs to give to whomever, whenever, and wherever they chose.

The punishment for trying to take The Gift, without the woman offering you The Gift first, was immediate death.

Fortunately for the men, women were so generous with The Gift that rape was virtually obsolete.

To fall in love as we do in our culture today, to obsess over one particular female, to want to keep her from sharing The Gift with anyone other than you, was an aberration abhorrent to all healthy sane Indian men, and women.

At the first sign of such spiritual and mental disorder, a Shaman was called in to perform exorcisms, healing rituals, and to cure the deviant.

During the UCLA survey of 1980 the most commonly reported apparition was that of Sum Yet Ho, the last Chief of all the tribes from Panama to Alaska this side of the Rockies. Men were not allowed to enter the women's area at the sacred birthing pools where women gave live birth to their Bear Spirit babies in the sacred water of the springs. Sum Yet Ho, whose name means Mighty Strong Right Arm, more or less, and all the Chiefs of Chiefs before him were the exceptions to that rule.

King Sum Yet Ho was not only allowed there, his presence was a great boon, and a blessing. Sum Yet Ho's presence was required, as it had been required of all the Chief of Chiefs, during the month of July, nine months after the Bear Sacrifice, when the royal Indian women gave birth to between 3,500 and 5,500 babies. All at the same time.

Babies born with birth defects were immediately sacrificed.

In Sonoma, the Indians received their souls, their names, and their assigned life-partners at the age of four. Marriage had nothing to do with sex. This was also the age at which they became exempt from the child sacrifices that occurred in times of extreme famine.

Adult sacrifice was practiced, but not in The Sacred Valley. Those ceremonies were carried out up in Santa Rosa, where the Fountain Grove property is today.

The child sacrifices took place in Saint Helena, and this is the origin of the name given to the area by the Spanish, "Carne Humana". It means "Flesh of Humans". This Spanish name can still be seen on the original Spanish land grants, and old property deeds.

The sacrifice of all children under the age of four immediately reduced the number of mouths to feed. It was a powerful blood sacrifice to the gods. And it provided an instant source of protein.

Mothers grieved, but they also believed that by consuming the flesh of their child, the child would be reborn as a part of their next baby.
Of course, if you work for the State, even as a volunteer, you are not allowed to say any of these things. The winners rewrite history.

When you walk along the area behind the Sonoma Mission's adobe wall, you may feel your feet, legs, and solar plexus become heavy, and your movement may become sluggish. There is a strong groundward pull here. You may experience an overwhelming desire to sit down. Most people do.

Indians in Sonoma never associated pregnancy with The Gift. Sex had nothing to do with marriage, because you were married at the age of four. An Indian woman could give The Gift to whomever she chose, according to how the Spirit of The Turquoise Maiden moved her.

A woman so inclined could even give The Gift to her husband.

The one thing that most upset the Catholic Padres, aside from the omnipresent practice of cannibalism, was the way women gave the Gift so generously, and to so many men. They gave it to their brothers, their sons, their uncles, their cousins, and even to strangers.

Baby making was a special thing that women did all by themselves with The Creator Spirit. So pervasive was this belief that there was no word for "Father" in the Indian language. The only word they had was "Uncle".

Each man in Sonoma, each man in The Earth Place, or The Earth Village, had an equal responsibility to help raise every child with whom he came in contact. Ponder that.

What would life be like if we all did that, all over the world? What if we went out and lived as though we are truly 100% responsible for the welfare of every child we met?

"Whoa!" as Jason would say.

When a woman was ready to make a baby, she went up to the Baby Rocks, and carved out a little hole with a piece of antler, or obsidian. She saved the dust from the hole, mixed it with the sacred bear-fat, and used the mixture to paint a Tic-Tack-Toe symbol on her belly, with the middle square around her belly button. Moons would pass, and sure enough, sooner or later, she would have a baby!

No wonder the men worshipped the women.

Even today on the school playground, when little boys and little girls get into wordy battles of one-upmanship, the girls still stomp the yard and win the battle with this one devastating truth:

"I can make babies, and you can't."

What can a boy say to top that?

If you want to visit some authentic Indian Baby Rocks in the Sacred Valley of Sonoma, go to the East entrance of the Sonoma Mountain Cemetery at the top of Second Street East.

Up on the hill, to the left of the big white cross, is a white rectangle of concrete. That is a gravesite, but it was built there because of the Baby Rocks.

There are many more Baby Rocks further up the hill around the Schocken Quarry. If you decide to hike up there, wear comfortable shoes, sunscreen, a hat. Take a bottle of water and your cell phone, just in case.

Do not go up there during the really dry seasons. That is when the rattlesnakes come down from the wild for water. Go when the grass is green.

Baby Rocks look volcanic, and sometimes they are volcanic, but they are not necessarily volcanic. They look volcanic because of all the holes. But ladies must be careful up there. Indian legend has it that you can get pregnant just by standing next to a Baby Rock.

About The Author

Carla Heine lives in the town of Sonoma, California, the spiritual heart of Sonoma's Wine Country. "Sonoma Ghosts" is a series based on the mysterious buildings and haunted sites in Sonoma. Many are open to the public, and afford visitors an opportunity to test, or develop their own psychic sensitivity in well-established haunts.

KSVY 91.3FM has aired Carla's radio show "Strange Wine – History and the Paranormal in the Valley of the Moon" from 11:00pm to midnight every Saturday night, for over five years. Podcasts are at: www.ksvy.org

NBC's national show "In Wine Country" toured Sonoma with Carla Heine as a featured guest. To see the Podcast on the Internet, Google www.inwinecountry.com, and enter: Is Sonoma Haunted.

Her first You Tube video is a free mini-tour of Sonoma's haunted places, directed and videoed by filmmaker Kelly Whalen, for the international video travel site TurnHere.com. Just Google "Haunted Sonoma".

Carla is deeply grateful to Sonoma, her family, her friends, her mentors, and each and every one of her students, both the living and the dead, for enriching her life exponentially with their infinite tolerance and enthusiastic support.

Oral history, and oral traditions have been known to morph with time, so if you have knowledge you can share to iron out the wrinkles time has wrought, please e-mail Carla at : sonomaghosts@hotmail,com.

Carla lives in Sonoma with her retired husband, John Mirsberger, a former Marine from New York City, on Blue Wing Drive, South of the Sonoma Mountain Cemetery. They have very quiet neighbors, and a preternaturally sensitive Jack Russell Terrier named Jake.

Made in the USA
Charleston, SC
26 March 2014